Waterfalls
& Gibbon Calls

Exploring Khao Sok National Park

Thom Henley

CONTENTS

Part IV Khao Sok Interpretive Trail

DEDICATION

This book is dedicated to His Royal Majesty King Bhumibol Aduladej.

It is our hope that His Majesty's earnest and urgent message of conservation will reach the heart of every Thai and foreigner who enters this remarkable forest.

Long live Khao Sok and all the National Parks and protected areas of Thailand.

LONG LIVE THE KING!

HOW TO USE THIS BOOK

For many years now travelers to Khao Sok National Park have been writing in the park's "Visitor's Comments" book: "Please, give us some information!" While this book does not pretend to be the definitive work on a park as widely diverse and complex as Khao Sok, it does offer a humble starting point.

How you use this book depends on what you want from it. If you're in a distant land contemplating your next adventure holiday, the photos, directions and lodge listings, suggested itineraries, and health & safety tips in the Part III "Visitor's Guide" might prove most useful.

If you're already at Khao Sok and looking for an easy hike or a full-day outing, the "Park Highlights" in Part II of this book and the feature maps should be of interest.

If you're a student or naturalist unfamiliar with the Southeast Asian tropical forest, the "Interpretive Trail Guide" in Part IV can serve as a nice introduction.

A serious scientist, birder or naturalist might find the check list for "Bird, Mammal, Reptile and Amphibian" species and the "Wildlife Tracks" pages most useful.

Anyone interested in history, both human and natural, and curious how this area evolved and ultimately became a national park, should find Part I, the opening section of the book, quite intriguing.

However you use this book – enjoy it, and pass it on for others to use. It's difficult to get recycled paper in Thailand.

INTRODUCTION

Whether you are on armchair explorer vicariously visiting Khao Sok or a rugged adventurer about to embark on a trek traversing the park's uncharted terrain, you are about to enter part of the oldest and richest terrestial ecosystem on Earth.

The world has spared few places as wild, wonderful or wildly diverse as Khao Sok National Park. Together with two wildlife sanctuaries (Klong Saen & Klong Nakkha) and two adjacent national parks (Sri Phangnga and Klong Phanom), Khao Sok is part of the largest protected area in South Thailand. At 4,400 sq.km, it is larger in size than Malaysia's Taman Negara National Park (4,362 sq.km), Indonesia's Gunung Leuser National Park (900 sq.km) and Sarawak's Mulu National Park (528 sq.km). Khao Sok is in fact one of Southeast Asia's most vital wildlife habitats.

By virtue of elimination these areas have become critical refuges, oases of life in landscapes that are now comparative biological deserts of oil palm and rubber plantations and logged over scrublands.

Khao Sok, and the few places like it, stand apart in Southeast Asia's geography of hope – hope for the region's last remaining wildlife, the world's greatest diversity of plant life, and last but not least, hope for the human spirit.

It is wonderful to watch Khao Sok cast its spell on people..... those magical mornings when the world seems new like the dawn of time and gibbon songs echo in the morning mist. There is the sheer joy of plunging into some of the coolest and cleanest rivers in Thailand at the base of a private waterfall. There's excitement when a flock of feeding hornbills compete for the same fig tree with more species of birds and small mammals than exist in many countries.

There are those magic moments when the whole world seems green in every conceivable shade and every conceivable shape, then suddenly one comes upon an 80 cm red blossom bursting from the ground – rafflesia – one of the largest flowers on Earth.

There is the power of tropical thunder storms, deluges of rain and raging rivers in this the wettest region of the Kingdom. One seeks shelter under an umbrella-shaped palm blade only to discover it's a new species and the rarest palm on Earth.

And there is the spark of danger, the remote but ever-present possibility that one might come face to face with the largest cat on Earth – that orange and black striped phantom that barely survives now in a world that has become all too tame for tigers.

These are images Khao Sok indelibly etches in the minds of those who know her intimately, those who make only a short acquaintance and those who see her only in the mind's eye. In a world changing in every way with unprecedented speed, it is comforting to know that there are such places, vast, untrammeled wildlands with mysteries so deep we may never fully fanthom them.

It is easy for visitors to Asia to be awed by the grandeur and antiquity of great human achievements – like Angkor Wat in Cambodia. As you explore Khao Sok's tropical forest try to remind yourself that this in Nature's greatest achievement – it's 200,000 times older than Angkor Wat, and more importantly, it's still alive, functioning, and evolving.

PART I
Khao Sok's History

NATURAL HISTORY OF KHAO SOK

Khao Sok National Park straddles the central mountain range which forms the backbone of the Thai / Malay peninsula and is located just south of the Isthmus of Kra, the peninsula's narrow neck. Monsoon rains sweep into these mountains from both the Gulf of Thailand in the east and the Andaman Sea / Indian Ocean in the west, resulting in this being Thailand's wettest area with 3,500 mm of rain recorded annually. Although rain falls in every month of the year, December to April is the driest period with May to November receiving a deluge.

Khao Sok has a complex but fascinating geological history. During the Carboniferous Period (345-280 million years ago), pebbly mudstones and sandstones of the Kaeng Krachan Formation were deposited on the edge of a deep ocean basin. As sediments were washed down from the ancient landmass of Shan-Thai, they accumulated around a delta system (similar to that seen in the Mississippi Delta today). These sediments built up into unstable deposits that periodically avalanched down the basin edge. Over the millions of years of the Carboniferous, the basin was filled with sediment as Shan-Thai landmass was heavily eroded. This caused the sea to be shallower and warmer, conditions which allowed for corals and other organisms to thrive.

It was during this period (280-225 million years ago) that the Permian limestone was deposited. Fossil remains found in the rock suggest a warm quiet sea and a coral reef (five times longer than the Great Barrier Reef) which stretched from China to Borneo.

In time this marine ecosystem became deeply buried under new sediment which created immense pressure resulting in the limestone rock we see here today.

While still deeply buried, granite intruded into the Carboniferous rocks in the form of large magmatic bodies. It was formed when the ancient Indian landmass slid under the Shan-Thai landmass. As the rock was pushed to great depths it melted and the molten rocks, being less dense, floated up like oil in water to intrude into the Carboniferous rocks. Chemicals in the hot magma mixed with water and chemicals from the sedimentary rocks to produce a "soup" rich in tin and tungsten, which solidified along the top of the granite. (It was these rich mineral deposits which attracted miners to Khao Sok in the 1960's - 70's to prospect for tin along the northern slopes of the Sok River).

In the Cenozoic Period (0-66 million years ago), all the rocks of the Khao Sok area were subjected to massive forces when the Indian plate crashed into the Eurasian plate, forming the Himalayas. The whole of Thailand was rotated clockwise and moved southeastwards as the Himalayan mountains rose. The rocks were uplifted, folded and faulted, and subsequently eroded.

Khao Sok's lofty karst formations, viewed from Cheow Lan Lake (pages 10-11, 13-14), present one of the most stunning landscapes in the world. They are uplifted and heavily weathered limestone crags that were part of an ancient coral reef 225-280 million years ago.

TOWERING LIMESTONE: *The twin peaks of Khao Serow (top) are the highest in the park and frequently wreathed in cloud. Karst formations in excess of 900 meters are almost unheard of anywhere else. The Tourism Authority of Thailand is now promoting Cheow Lan Lake as Thailand's Guilin -- a karst area of southern China long considered the most beautiful place in the world.*

The last Ice Age played a significant role in the formation of Khao Sok's landscape even though this area was not glaciated. Water trapped in the enlarged polar caps caused the sea level to fall, rejuvenating the fluvial systems and producing greater erosion. As the polar ice caps melted back at the close of the Ice Age, sea levels rose again and the process of erosion was slowed resulting in the smaller meandering rivers and dramatic topography we see here now.

Today Khao Sok's low forest-clad mountains made up of mudstone and siltstone from the Permian Carboniferous period rise to elevations averaging 300 - 600 m above sea level. These are bisected by a north-south range of limestone outcrops called karsts that tower to 960 m at the highest point in the park.

Khao Sok's dramatic karst topography also occurs in Guilin, China, Halong Bay, Vietnam, Vang Vieng Laos, Phangnga Bay and Krabi Thailand, and Sarawak, Borneo. It is the remnant of an ancient coral reef system that stretched across the shallow seas of Southeast Asia in the Permian period.

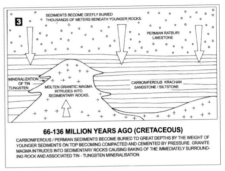

66-136 MILLION YEARS AGO (CRETACEOUS)
CARBONIFEROUS / PERMIAN SEDIMENTS BECOME BURIED TO GREAT DEPTHS BY THE WEIGHT OF YOUNGER SEDIMENTS ON TOP BECOMING COMPACTED AND CEMENTED BY PRESSURE. GRANITE MAGMA INTRUDES INTO SEDIMENTARY ROCKS CAUSING BAKING OF THE IMMEDIATELY SURROUNDING ROCK AND ASSOCIATED TIN - TUNGSTEN MINERALISATION.

280-345 MILLION YEARS AGO (CARBONIFEROUS)
KAENG KRACHEN SANDSTONE / MUDSTONE FORMATION IS LAID DOWN AS MARINE TURBIDITE DEPOSITS THROUGH HEAVY PROCESS OF EROSION.

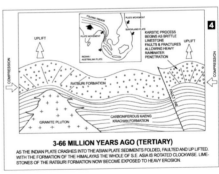

3-66 MILLION YEARS AGO (TERTIARY)
AS THE INDIAN PLATE CRASHES INTO THE ASIAN PLATE SEDIMENTS FOLDED, FAULTED AND UP LIFTED. WITH THE FORMATION OF THE HIMALAYAS THE WHOLE OF S.E. ASIA IS ROTATED CLOCKWISE. LIMESTONES OF THE RATBURI FORMATION NOW BECOME EXPOSED TO HEAVY EROSION.

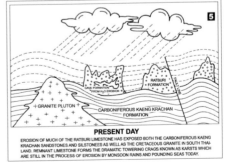

225-280 MILLION YEARS AGO (PERMIAN)
THE RATBURI LIMESTONE FORMATION IS DEPOSITED. FOSSILS FOUND WITHIN THE LIMESTONE SUGGEST A WARM, SHALLOW SEA FAVORABLE FOR CORAL REEF GROWTH.

PRESENT DAY
EROSION OF MUCH OF THE RATBURI LIMESTONE HAS EXPOSED BOTH THE CARBONIFEROUS KAENG KRACHAN SANDSTONES AND SILSTONEES AS WELL AS THE CRETACEOUS GRANITE IN SOUTH THAILAND. REMNANT LIMESTONE FORMS THE DRAMATIC TOWERING CRAGS KNOWN AS KARSTS WHICH ARE STILL IN THE PROCESS OF EROSION BY MONSOON RAINS AND POUNDING SEAS TODAY.

UNIQUELY KHAO SOK: *Towering to elevations of 960 meters, the spectacular karsts of Khao Sok **1** are among the highest limestone crags in the world. Khao Sok's endermic Rafflesia Kerri Meijer is found here and nowhere else. Once a year this parasitic plant swells to a bud the size of a soccer ball **2**, before bursting open into a 80 cm. bloom **3**. Palm pralahoo **4**, restricted to limestone cliffs and palm langkow **5** growing deep in the forest, are other plants unique to Khao Sok.*

Vegetation on limestone karsts must be able to withstand desiccation during dry seasons, almost a complete lack of soil, and severe exposure to the elements. Animals,too, need special adaptations to live in such an environment. The sure-footed serow, a goat-antelope, is one of the few large mammals that habitate in karst environments.

Approximately 15% of Khao Sok's landscape is made up of lime-stone crag vegetation. Other forest types include : rainforest plains 27%, rainforest foothills 40%, submontane lowland scrub 15% and lowland rainforest (600-1,000m) 3%.

When it comes to classifying forest types and forest structure in neat categories science sometimes finds the world to be considerably more complex than the categories would seem to indicate. Khao Sok, for instance, has features of both tropical evergreen forest and tropical rainforest; it meets part of the definitions of both. The interchangeable use of these names in this book is presented deliberately to further the debate.

The Khao Sok rainforest, techni-cally a "tropical evergreen forest", is a remnant of a 160 million year old forest ecosystem – one much older and richer than the Amazon or the rainforests of central Africa. The reasons for this appear fourfold :

1. The Sunda shelf which con-tains South Thailand, the Malay penin-sula, Sumatra, Java, Bali and Borneo, all remained geologically stable on the equator for tens of millions of years while other continental masses were shifting on plates, entering different climatic zones in relation to the Earth's poles. Because of this unusual stability tropical rainforests existed in the Khao Sok region during the Tertiary Period, the last geological era.

2. Another reason for the antiq-uity and complexity of this ecosystem is that it was climatically unaffected by the Ice Ages which altered so much of Eurasia's vegetation. At a time when much of the world's fresh water was locked in ice, the Amazon and Africa's Congo river basin desiccated and became largely dry-land savannah rather than rainforest. Southeast Asia had a distinct geographical advantage by not being at the center of a continental land mass. Composed of thousands of islands and a narrow peninsula surrounded by water there was sufficient moisture and humidity here for rainforests to continue to flourish.

3. The third factor influencing this region's great biological diversity is also a result of the Ice Age. During the Pleistocene Epoch there were times when the sea level was 180 meters lower than today. This resulted in a vast land bridge across the shallow Sunda shelf linking the Malay peninsula with the great islands of Borneo, Sumatra and Java. This allowed for easy interchange of species that had evolved in isolation. Southeast Asia was thus endowed with unsurpassed biological riches: hundreds of species of mammals, more than 1,500 species of birds and well over 1,000 species of reptiles and amphibians.

NEW DISCOVERIES: *Never before documented, Great hornbills at Khao Sok have taken to nesting inside cliff faces, instead of the customary tree chamber. A male guards over the nest site while perched on a nearby branch* **6**. *Balancing on its spread tail* **7** *it regurgitates figs one by one* **8**, *then feeds them to its enclosed mate through the small opening in the mud and excrement plaster* **9** *which walls off the nest chamber (arrow →).*

4. There is yet another interesting factor affecting Khao Sok's species diversity. A distinct biological boundary between the Indo-Chinese and Sundaic sub-regions is located at the Isthmus of Kra, just north of the Khao Sok National Park boundary. Khao Sok then lies in the transition zone between these two vast subregions and is blessed with species from both areas.

The forests of Khao Sok are dense, stratified structures dominated by towering emergent trees which are often supported by buttress roots. The upper and lower canopy levels, or middle story of the forest, is joined together vertically and horizontally by an aerial tangle of woody liana vines. The understory is made up of many species of palms, tree saplings and a predominance of bamboo. Some of the plant species found here are endemic and extremely rare such as two palm specie: "langkow" and "mack pralahoo", and "bua poot", a new species of rafflesia, which parasitically lives on certain ground-loving lianas.

The botanical richness of the region, the abundance of fresh water and the protection offered by extremely rugged terrain make Khao Sok prime habitat for many species of wildlife. Together with the wildlife sanctuaries of Klong Saeng and Klong Nakha located to the north of Khao Sok, Sri Phang nga National Park to the west, and Klong Phanom, National Park to the south, this is the largest protected forest area in southern Thailand and the only viable habitat for mammals needing extensive tracts of virgin forest for their survival.

While the wildlife inventories for Khao Sok are far from complete the number of species confirmed to date include 48 species of mammals and 311 species of birds. The classification of reptiles, amphibians, insects and plants has barely begun. Part V of this book provides a check list for bird, mammal, reptile and amphibian species "confirmed" or "expected" at Khao Sok according to a Chiang Mai University's mass data base.

ON-GOING RESEARCH: *New research at Khao Sok, and its adjacent parks and wildlife sanctuaries is constantly documenting new species of birds, mammals, amphibians, reptiles and insects.*

BIRDS : *Among Khao Sok's 311 confirmed species of birds are:*
1 Rhinocerous hornbill,   2 Great hornbill, 3 Crested Serpent-eagle,
4 Collared scops owls, 5 Malayan peacock pheasant, 6 Great argus pheasant

MAMMALS: *Thailand supports 6% of all mammal species on Earth, and Khao Sok is especially rich in species. Among it's 48 confirmed species are : **1** Leopard cat. **2** Common flying fox, **3** Asiatic black bear, **4** Long-tail macaque, **5** Asian elephant, **6** Barking deer*

KHAO SOK'S HUMAN HISTORY

The Malay Peninsula and southern Thailand present one of the most complex human migration routes in the world. The few sites that have had archeological work done reveal layer upon layer of human use and occupation from so many different periods and different cultures that analysis is difficult. Pre-historic cave paintings and burial sites present us with even more mysteries.

No one knows for certain whether the area that is now Khao Sok National Park was occupied by humans in the pre-historic past. It is rugged land remote from the well-traveled coast, but it is also amazingly rich in wild fruit and meat and contains countless caves for human habitation. Stone age peoples may well have occupied these lands until quite recently.

The Khao Sok area was, in all likelihood, home to nomadic forest dwelling tribes similar to the Mani – the last bands of hunter-gatherer forest peoples still surviving in the Trang mountains and near the border of Thailand and Malaysia. At the oldest known human habitation site in Southeast Asia, the Niah Caves in northern Borneo, archeologists have dated human skulls back 37,000 years and found evidence of 50,000 year old habitation. The similarity of extensive cave systems and rich rainforest, and the fact that Khao Sok and Borneo were connected by a land bridge during the last great Ice Age make prehistoric occupation of this area more than mere conjecture.

The first historic accounts of people residing in the Khao Sok area date back to the reign of King Rama II in the later part of the 18th century. When the Burmese attacked the coastal towns of Takuapa, Takua Toong and Talang (Phuket) the survivors fled inland through the vast forest, crossing rivers and mountains, in fear of their lives. One group made their way as far as Khao Sok.

The people, in time, became comfortable with their exile and in addition to hunting, fishing, and gathering wild fruits and greens from the forest they began to clear land for the cultivation of rice, vegetables and domestic fruit. The land here was surprisingly fertile and rainfall more than adequate for the new settlement to flourish. Glowing reports spread of rivers teeming with fish and wild cattle, deer and boar in abundance. More settlers came; the forest was cut further and further back as the population grew and prospered. Were it not for a twist of fate the Khao Sok forest may well have gone the way of most forests in Thailand.

In the Thai calendar year 2487 (1944) a deadly epidemic struck the Khao Sok settlement and ravaged the population. The few survivors once again fled for their lives. The abandoned village became known as Ban Sop, Village of the Dead. Some older inhabitants of the Khao Sok region maintain that this morbid name comes from the neighboring Pantoorat (Giant) mountain, also known as Khao Sop, "Corpse Mountain", as it is said to resemble the prayer position a body is laid in for funeral rites. The name Khao Sok is meant to be a less sinister version of Khao Sop.

The village of Ban Sop remained isolated from the outside world, cut off by dense forest, until 1961 when the Mahat Thai company cut the first road connecting Phun Phin in Surat Thani Province with Takuapa in Phangnga Province.

About 1,000 workers were brought in to build the road and they located their construction camp near Pantoorat Mountain. The old village of Ban Sok had new life but the forest and animals faced unprecedented threats. Modern weapons allowed the construction workers to take a terrible toll on the wildlife. The new road brought a flood of eager settlers from the provinces of Songkhla, Nakhorn Sri Thammarat, Chumpon, and Prachuab Khiri Khan who began to cut, clear and claim the richest wildlife habitat, the lowland forest, as their own.

Concessions were soon obtained from the government for the mining of tin ore and commercial logging. Logging roads began to penetrate Khao Sok's vast wilderness and the Sok River flowed brown with runoff from mining. Once again it appeared that the great riches of this region would be quickly looted. Then yet another twist of fate brought a measure of relief.

In the late 1970's many Thai students frustrated with attempts to bring about meaningful change in their government joined communist insurgency groups and fled into some of the last remnants of Thailand's forests. Khao Sok offered the perfect hideout. With their stronghold in the rugged karst mountains of the present Cheow Lan Lake site, they were able to thwart all attempts at military intervention. From 1975 to 1982, during a period in which logging companies were running riot throughout Thailand, the insurgency groups held all incursions into their occupied areas at bay. Their goal was defense rather than conservation but their seven year period of occupation was crucial to Khao Sok's protection.

During the period of communist insurgency and occupation the government took a look at the Khao Sok region for other than military reasons. An aerial survey in 1971 had already shown that the mountain streams around Khao Sok are part of the largest watershed in southern Thailand, and that the forest was still largely intact. Both the National Parks Division and EGAT (the Electricity Generating Authority of Thailand) now took a keen interest. The National Park Division assigned officers to survey the area. Their report confirmed the rich biodiversity of flora and fauna, several rare types of vegetation and many outstanding features: spectacular

STONE AGE PEOPLES: *Though they have been swept from history, Khao Sok was likely home to forest dwelling bands of nomads much like the Mani who still hunt with blowpipers* **1,** *eat roasted jungle tubers* **2,** *and live in simple shelters* **3** *in Thailand's southern-most forests today.*

limestone mountains, cliffs, caves, rivers and many waterfalls.

It was decided that all logging and mining practices must stop and the process of establishing Khao Sok as a National Park was begun. The Park Division marked out the boundaries of the park south from the Pasaeng and Yee rivers. On the 22nd of December 1980, Khao Sok was formally established as Thailand's 22nd National Park covering an area of 645.52 sq.km.

The ink was barely dry on the entitlement paper when EGAT forever altered the park's boundaries with the daming and flooding of the Pasaeng River. Rachabrapah Dam, 95 m high and 700 m long, was constructed of shale and clay across the Pasaeng River in 1982 to create a massive 165 sq.km. reservoir to generate hydroelectric power. The longest free-flowing river in south Thailand and the boundaries of a national park were compromised to guarantee a reliable source of power to the South's rapidly developing centers of trade, commerce and tourism. It was a disaster for wildlife.

As the lake waters slowly rose EGAT funded the largest wildlife rescue operation ever undertaken in south Thailand. It was led by Thailand's leading conservationist, the late Serb Nakhasathien, who later took his own life to bring attention to the plight of the Kingdom's wildlife.

PARADISE LOST: *Great treasures were lost with the flooding of Khao Sok's lowland forest. Stunningly beautiful caves and massive trees were submerged with the rising dam waters. Gibbons, langurs and other animals, that will not cross water, became trapped on small islands losing the large territories they need to survive. Deer, tapir and elephant, though they can swim, lost their richest foraging grounds. Fruit-eating bats and birds, though they can fly, lost much of their food base when all of the lowland trees were cut.*

FLOODED LOWLANDS: *The tops of huge emergent trees, rising above the flood waters of Cheow Lan Reservoir, stand as stark reminders of Khao Sok's rich rainforest that once covered the lowlands. The deep, oxygen-deficient waters of the reservoir were not suitable to the fish that once lived here. Fifty-two native species perished, but new species were introduced to support a local fishery.*

The Wildlife Conservation Division had determined that no fewer than 237 wild animal species would be impacted by the development. The plan was to capture and relocate animals that would become trapped on the more than 100 islands which would be created by the rising waters, and relocate them above the 100 m elevation of the mainland shore. The rescue operation relocated 1,364 birds, mammals and reptiles.

Wildlife "rescue" operations, unfortunately, do more to soothe our sense of guilt than serve or save wildlife. Many animals died of stress and shock at being captured and handled. Most "rescued" animals were relocated to ranges already overcrowded with refugee species who had arrived there on their own and out of necessity.

A nesting pair of Storms stork (Ciconia stormi) were found in the Klong Mon tributary of the Pasaeng River. This is the only known sighting of this marsh bird in all of Thailand. Later, as the dam waters rose, biologists reported a Storms stork nest with two young in a tall dipterocarp tree, presumably to escape the flooding. Storms stork has not been seen at Khao Sok since.

The impact of the dam is still being studied. Inbreeding of trapped populations that will not cross any body of water (like gibbons and langurs) is a serious problem. The reservoir has compounded the problem of patroling the park as poachers now have easy access by boat to the most remote corners of Khao Sok National Park and the adjacent wildlife sanctuaries. More than 200 fishermen make their business living on float houses (sometimes poaching wildlife) and catching for commercial purposes many fish species introduced to the huge artificial lake.

A total of 52 fish species were lost with the construction of the dam according to a 1995 World Bank study by Kasetsart University. Migratory fish unable to go upriver to spawn dwindled in numbers or went extinct. Other, non-migratory species, unable to survive in waters more than two meters deep due to temperature changes in deeper water, also perished. Biomass decay in reservoirs pollutes water and robs fish of oxygen.

In a world where the global population is predicted to double within this century, it will take real diligence to keep places like Khao Sok intact. The next chapter in Khao Sok National Park's history will be encouraging for all if the world can embrace a new value system which recognizes the rights and needs of species other than just ourselves.

Pua and Gao outside their shop near the park entrance gate.

A VOICE FROM THE "VILLAGE OF THE DEAD" (PUA SITIPONG)

Six decades ago a horrible epidemic swept the Ban Sok community; only eight out of 100 people survived. Khao Sok's last living memory of the great tragedy is a 81 year old, beetlenut chewing, shopkeeper who lives near the park gate, and who might just sell you a pineapple from her garden, if you're nice.

I had just settled into doing an interview with Khun Pua, something I'd been wanting to do for years, when a young *farang* roared up to the front of her shop on his motorcycle. In a cloud of dust and without the courtesy of a greeting he brazenly demanded : "How much are yer pineapples, Mate?" The old grey haired matriarch stopped cutting her beetlenut and lowered her spectacles to see what this latest plague to hit Khao Sok was all about. Pua, and Pua alone, had already seen it all. This sole survivor of the great Ban Sok epidemic had a story to tell before she passed from the world, if only someone cared to listen.

Pua Sitipong was born the second oldest of three siblings, Jaen, Puang and Pat, to a mother who had also been born at Ban Sok. It was a small village of thirty houses and only 100 residents, but it was a prosperous one. People raised pigs in pens beneath their elevated stilt houses and hiked them, two at a time on leashes, to the market in Takuapa. The amazing thing about this 40 km trek which crossed two mountain passes was that it was done in a single day – a mere ten hours! Backpackers returning exhausted from their 18 km hike to Ton Gloy Waterfall should *wai* very high to Khun Pua as they pass her house today.

There is another reason for reverence. Pua never left Ban Sok. When the epidemic struck the community, those who didn't perish fled for their lives. Pua's father, who was born in nearby Ramni, was a jungle doctor. He dug earthworms and stuffed them into a large green coconut which was then cooked in an open fire. Only the six members of his family would drink this bizarre concoction, but miraculously, his entire family were among the eight survivors.

Pua married a man ten years her junior, Khun Gao, who moved onto the family property with her when all the rest of her family eventually passed away or moved away from this "Village of the Dead." Gao was a hunter and he needed to be. Five times Gao shot tigers stalking up to his house to eat the family water buffalows, pigs, or sometimes, the pet dog. Python posed a greater danger to his livestock and many a pig that foraged in the forest at night was little more than a pig shaped lump in the body of a happy python by dawn. No one in Ban Sok ever lost their life to a wild animal Gao says, but twenty years ago a man from Ban Tahan, just 10 km. west of Ban Sok, was attacked and eaten by a tiger as he was bent over scraping the thorny spines from rattan vine.

Pua and Gao defended themselves from attacks, but learned to live with the many animals that knew Khao Sok as home before too many humans made it theirs. They would wake at dawn to huge flocks of hornbills, hear gibbons calling from every direction and have to chase the Malay sun bears and Asiatic black bears out of their orchards and pineapple patch. Today, nearly two decades after the national park was created to protect the remaining animals, Gao notes their continued demise. "Too many people shoot the animals to sell them in the market", Gao says, "and too many tourists hiking the trails drive the remaining wildlife further and further away." "The animals can't trust people, they run away," Pua adds.

Pua and Gao's greatest lament is that in another 20 years there won't be any wild animals, that the history of this extraordinary region bursting with life will be only a memory they carry to their graves with them

It is not often a single couple carry in their minds and their hearts the last living memory of a healthy forest and the once healthy community that flourished there. Show a little reverence when you buy their pineapples.

KHAO SOK'S LAST COMMUNIST
(WANO TIPAVRAT)

Thirty-five years ago 170 university students fled for their lives into the deepest recesses of Khao Sok's caves. For eight years they held the Thai army and the logging companies at bay. Inadvertently they not only saved Khao Sok's forests but brought more protection to the region's wildlife than the national park designation does today.

I was engaged in an interview with Khun Pua, the oldest survivor of Ban Sok, and enquiring about Khao Sok's period of communist insurgency when my translator, Nit (Anitsak Chanyoo) got excited: "Thom, still have one communist live here. You want to meet?" It was already dusk and the evening dry season cicadas were setting off an ear splitting din as we drove the bumpy dirt road into a deep hidden corner of the Sok River Valley. Parking Nit's pick up truck, we still had to hike a foot path to find the reclusive home of Nit's friend Amnat, Khao Sok's last resident of the student insurgency days. Amnat's wife and children were enjoying the cool evening respite from the tiled porch of their well-built home. It seemed a far cry from being hunkered down in bunkers while 105 mm bullets rained from the skies. There was a story here only Amnat could tell.

Forty-three years old, dark and good looking, Amnat's eyes came alive when he recalled four of his teen years living in Khao Sok's most remote reaches. A student protest against the military government October 6th, 1976 resulted in a Bangkok massacre of students from Thamarsat, Ramkamhaeng and Juralongkorn Universities. As military helicopters rained death from the skies on the unarmed protestors, an unknown number died and hundreds of others fled for their lives. "If they stayed in Bangkok they died," Amnat said matter-of-factly.

Amnat was born Wano Tipavrat in Suratthani but received his code name of "Amnat" at a Communist Army Camp before going to Khao Sok. He was one of 170 students who suddenly found themselves far removed from the privileged halls of academia. They were all branded "communists" by the government of the country they had been studying to serve.

Amnat was posted at the entrance to Namtaloo Cave which was the hospital, while Seroo Cave served as military command post. Under the concealment of a huge Grandiflora tree (still standing today) the students erected their primitive infirmary. Bamboo platforms elevated a foot off the ground served as beds while camouflaged painted tarps were suspended from sapling frames to shed the torrential monsoon rains, provide shade and, most of all, offer concealment from Thai Army spotter helicopters. Whenever the army did think they had a fix on the students positions they'd fire their mortars and the teenagers would flee to the safety of Namtaloo Cave. There was even a stone bunker built above the cave entrance (still visible today) where a student sniper could hold off advancing ground troops while the other students escaped through the 500 m deep cave tunnel out the back side of the mountain.

Few backpackers today, who hike through this cave on an adventure of a lifetime, realize how their experience pales compared to that of Amnat and his teenage compatriots.

This was not some "Top Gun"/ "Rambo"-like undertaking. Thirty percent of the student army were girls. All of these teenagers could pose as civilians at anytime and even sell their produce at the local markets. They purchased food, medicines and even M-16 and AKA automatic weapons from military brass always out to make a buck. Amnat's special task was creating a security perimeter around the hospital area of Namtaloo Cave. He filled PCP pipe with TNT and buried it in the ground, just below the surface. A trip wire was rigged to the bomb, and attatched to a contact point on a concealed battery. Woe to the unwary. (Fortunately for back packers the batteries should be defunct today ; but don't take my word on it.)

COMMUNIST HIDEOUTS: *A huge tree with part of its flarred root base cut away 1, once suprised many hikers along the Namtaloo Cave Trail. It secretly marked the small, hidden exit of this "Communist" defense cave. (The tree has recently been toppled by a storm.) The much larger entrance 2 is distinguished by a huge, fang-like stalactite.*

Malaria was as grave a threat to the students lives as were combat wounds, but medicine was always available and with trained student doctors on hand, no one died of any disease. Miraculously, only one student was killed during the entire period of occupation. He was on a standard patrol mission near the highway when he encountered the Thai Army. The student opened fire, they returned fire and he was killed. Some years later Amnat returned to the jungle grave site to retrieve the boy's bones for his family.

For eight years the "communists" lived a largely self-contained life deep in the forests of Khao Sok. They cleared areas for swidden rice cultivation near Ao Din Daeng and Tone Tuey. They even built a water-powered rice mill beside the creek. They grew lemons, coffee, bettlenut, coconuts, bananas, mangos, durian and other fruits. They raised pigs and chickens and caught fish as an additional protein supplement, but remarkably, they never hunted the abundant wild game. Strict orders from their Commanding Officer forbade the shooting of animals, and anyone violating this order was given a stern warning followed by dismissal if the warning went unheeded. This was not a conservation strategy, rather a survival one. Any unnecessary gun fire gave away the students' positions to the Thai Army, and any shooting of game by the Army gave away their position to the students. Not even a wildlife poacher would dare to enter this combat zone. It was a stalemate and the wildlife were the winners; so was the forest. The students couldn't risk the noise of a chainsaw so they were forbidden; they couldn't risk a logging road penetrating into the forest for the army to follow, so they held the loggers at bay.

It is a strange irony how these 170 "communist" students not only saved Khao Sok's forests so that it could later qualify for park status, but accorded Khao Sok's wildlife the most protection it has had in the entire Twentieth Century. There was a happy ending for the students too. A change of government brought an unconditional amnesty for the rebels and little by little they started finding their way back home. According to Amnat, the last "communist" left Namtaloo Cave in 1989, just as the first tourists were starting to arrive.

There are few reminders today of that historic era. Tourists travel to Namtaloo Cave today across a dam reservoir, riding in boats 50-100 meters above the trails the students followed. A few bunker holes are visible beside the Namtaloo trail and sometimes a cache is found (200 liter plastic bins containing rice, salt and garlic) which can supplement a campers rations, but for the most part eight years of Khao Sok's history have nearly been swept away.

Khun Wano is still known as Amnat by those who know him well, and he still adheres to higher causes. Amnat was the first "Sunpet Raka", the big boss of the new Klong Phanom National Park which lies adjacent to Khao Sok National Park. It somehow seems appropriate that while the Khao Sok trails are bursting at the seams with visitors, just across the road in Klong Phanom National Park, Amnat still has his hideaways.

STUDENT SANCTUARIES: *Throughout South Thailand student protestors, labeled communists in the 1970's, sought sanctuary in the last unlogged forests. Today the same bush skills that helped the rebels survive, like cooking food in bamboo, are shared with adventure tourists.*

OLYMPIC GOLD BUNGALOW

Olympic silver medalist Worapoj Petchkoom stands on the winner's podium at the 2004 Athens Olympics biting his lower lip to conceal his disappointment. One step above him, following a very close decision, stands the 54 kg gold medalist in boxing receiving the medal Worapoj reserved in his mind for himself.

That iconic image now graces a demonstration boxing stage in the restaurant of Khao Sok's most unlikely bungalow business. Instead of adorning himself in gold, driving flash cars and catering to advertising contracts, as do many champions, Worapoj used his Olympic earnings and fame to help his Khao Sok subsistence farming family enter the tourism business.

Building a small 5-room resort on two rai of land his father already owned Worapoj has created employment for five of his seven siblings. Born the fifth child in a family of eight, Worapoj started boxing Muay Thai at age 10. His bouts in Suratthani, Krabi and Phuket were successful enough to earn him a scholarship to the National Sporting School in Ubon at age 14 where he shifted his style to Western boxing and was assigned a Cuban coach. The rest is history.

Visitors can find their way to Worapoj Resort by several signs along the highway showing the young Olympiad on the victory podium. A large covered boxing ring is the first facility you will see as you drive into the complex. Here Worapoj and his brothers teach up to 20 local youth boxing skills during their school breaks. The family provides this service free of charge, as Worapoj believes sporting activity and

having a goal in life is the best way for kids to build strong character, avoid drugs and be successful.

There is certainly no lack of discipline in Worapoj's life. At age 29 he has no wife or children and no time to socialize; he is still in training to capture that elusive Olympic gold. After securing silver in Athens and failing to reach the podium in Beijing in 2008, Worapoj defied the skeptics by becoming the only Thai to win a gold medal in boxing at the 2010 Asian Games.

While the odds do not favor the older athlete capturing Olympic gold in the 56 kg division in London in 2012, no one that knows Worapoj is counting him out. His Cinderella assent from Khao Sok rubber farmer to world stage combined with his dedication to family and community have already earned him gold in most people's minds.

FROM HUNTER TO ECO GUIDE, FATHER TO SON
(NIT & YOU CHANYOO)

One day Khao Sok's best elephant and tiger hunter put down his gun and dedicated his life to conservation. Today he's Khao Sok's top eco guide, or is it his son?

Born in Koh Samui, the second oldest of three boys, Anitsak Chanyoo, nicknamed "Nit" spent the first twenty years of his life working the family banana garden and coconut plantation. While his older and younger brothers went off to universities and became teachers and eventually head masters of local schools, Nit turned to the jungle for his education. The Chanyoo family had moved from Koh Samui to Khao Sok twenty eight years ago for no particular reason but to make a new garden. They acquired 18 rai of land which they cleared and planted in coconut, then later converted to rambutan.

Nit worked hard to support his mother but gardening in this remote region so far f rom major markets proved marginal. He turned to hunting Khao Sok's large mammals: elephant, bear, sambar deer, gaur and even tiger. Some of the hunting was considered self defense, like shooting tiger that ate the

pigs on his farm and one tiger that killed a villager. Bears raiding the fruit in his rambutan orchard met a similar fate. Sometimes Sambar deer and gaur were taken for meat, both to eat locally and to sell, but the big commercial venture was elephant hunting. Buyers in Suratthani were paying 3,000 baht per kilogram for elephant ivory and a single tusk could fetch 66,000 baht even back then. It took seven hunters working together to corner and kill a wild elephant, but the 132,000 baht they shared for the sale of the two tusks was the equivalent of half a year's salary for each of them.

Lucrative as the trade in ivory was, Nit's mother kept encouraging her son to stop hunting once Khao Sok was established as a national park in 1980. Nit was reminded of his mothers words one day as he watched the old matriarch of a herd of female elephants caring for their young calves. He put down his gun and never took it up again.

Today Nit at age 50 has become a teacher like his two brothers. Though he carries no letters after his name he is sought after by researchers and international scientists as Khao Sok's top tracker and most knowledgeable guide. A good deal of the information contained in this book is, in fact, a result of his teachings and years of friendship.

Nit started professional guiding eight years ago and says he is happier to show tourists the animals alive than he ever was when hunting them. Not all tourists react in the same way, he laughs. Some *"farang"* tourists who want to see tiger cry in fear if they ever actually encounter one. Thai tourists are different too, he says. When he spots Dusky langurs, (leaf monkeys) high in the branches, many Bangkok tourists want to know if he can make them langur curry.

Today Nit is one of Khao Sok's most dedicated conservationists. He meticulously picks up every speck of lifter or any cigarette butt he finds along the trails and he photo documents poacher activity to assist in park enforcement. "There's more trapping than hunting in the park now," Nit says: "It's safer." He recently photographed a serow, a goat antelope, with its leg broken in a poacher's trap. Locals sell the horn as a dagger lashed to the spurs of roosters in cock fighting and either eat or sell the meat, he says. There is growing evidence of major corruption in the illegal trade of wildlife parts from Khao Sok and Nit is not optimistic about the future of tiger, gaur, sambar deer and other mega fauna. "I think there will still be elephant here in twenty years time," he adds on a more upbeat note.

Impacts on the park's fauna come from every side. The commercial poaching has been exacerbated by the increase in local settlers. Poor people from Isaan (Northeast Thailand) come here to be laborers in the fruit planta-tions and hunt to supplement their low salaries. "They trap and eat everything," Nit notes: "pangolin, porcupine, lizards, cicadas and even scorpions." Foreign tourists also impact on the wildlife Nit believes. "There's too many bungalows now, several hundred people per day on the trails," he says: "The animals are moving further back leaving only spiders for people who want to see wildlife".

If there's a bright ray of hope in the future, Nit, like many fathers, sees it in his son. For twenty one years "You" has been at his fathers side learning about Khao Sok's rainforest from the most knowledgeable man alive. You is in other ways different from most kids his age born and raised in the Khao Sok area. "How can Khao Sok's wildlife be saved?" I asked the young man who now stands head and shoulders above his father. Without hesitating he laid out a three point program in perfect English. "Educate children from the youngest age in the schools," he replied. "Have a course for them to love the animal for protection... The young people must see the animal and think, oh, lovely animal, want to keep in the jungle always, not think, oh, good food, I want to eat it. You's second point is to put more national park staff on patrol, armed if necessary, to ward off potential poachers and ensure the animals' safety. Finally, he believes everybody at Khao Sok, residents and visitors alike, should have an orientation program of how to protect the park, and reduce their impacts upon it.

"What is your greatest concern?," I asked this articulate and bright young man who now wants to go around to local schools and start speaking on conser-vation to the students. "I worry that I will not be able to show my own children the animals in the wild my father has shown me. I worry that I will only be able to show them the photos in your book."

Mobile: *(66) 087 263 3062*
(66) 086 471 5411
E-mail: *adventureunlimited@gmail.com*

Note: *"You" worked with the Thai Nature Education program at local schools in 2003. See next pages.*

ECO EDUCATION: *Thai Nature Education, a program this book helps to support, has targeted every school surrounding Khao Sok National Park with environmental awareness programs. Slide lectures, songs, experiential games and traditional shadow puppet theater using animal puppets all help reinforce the conservation message.*
Local students have also been taken into the park to help conduct the first ever inventory and mapping of gibbon territories and hornbill nesting sites.

WILDLIFE GUARDIANS: *Surveying the shoreline of Cheow Lan for gibbon families, hornbill nest cavities and flying fox colonies is a huge but essential task. Through In Touch With Nature Education programs, the students learn the vital role these 'keystone' species play in seed dispersal. Lose these species and you lose much of the forest itself.*
Each student makes a pledge in writing of what action they will take to change local attitudes and their own behavior before accepting an embroidered patch. In doing so they become a fruit bat, hornbill, or "gibbon guardian" for life.

GETTING IT RIGHT

It takes a certain set of skills, a flair for style and a deep love of nature to build compatible within Khao Sok's lush setting. Fortunately, some Khao Sok bungalow operators have what it takes.

Born in Sakao, near the Cambodian border, and holding an Education degree from Sukhothai Thammathirat University, Chachirt Sukpraset (nicknamed Art), seems an unlikely person to be running a Khao Sok bungalow business. He has in fact been doing it longer, and better than most.

Art grew up in nature, and following his degree and a two-year teaching stint at an international school in Bangkok, his spirit was crying out to return to it. In 1986, just six years after Khao Sok was designated a national park, Art found himself at the doorstep of Dwalia Armstrong, the American expat that opened the park's first private bungalow business – Treetops Jungle Safari. Helping to oversee the construction of the lodge and tree-houses, and serving as General Manager for two years, gave Art a new and valuable education in the tourism industry.

Wanting a place of his own to build a house, Art purchased nearly 100-rai of land from Dwalia on the opposite bank of the Sok River. His home became known as Art's Jungle House, and it wasn't long before a few house guests expanded into a steady business. Art too had found an American expat to partner with, but as so often happens in business there was an eventual parting of ways. In 1994 Art started building his bungalow business all over again, claiming his part of the company land near the "monkey swimming hole". Art's Jungle House continued its business under the new name 'Our Jungle House,' while Art named his new establishment Art's Riverview Lodge.

The saying 'third time lucky' has never been truer than in Art's case. Having learned from building and operating two previous lodges, he now knew exactly what to do. Finding the balance between meeting people's comfort and not compromising the natural experience has always been Art's objective. For years he even refused to have electricity on his premises, preferring the jungle romance of soft candle light and lanterns. Eventually, Art gave in to guests requesting brighter lights to read by.

Tour groups now make up at least half of Art's business and he has expanded to 25 units ranging from tree houses to luxury riverside suites to meet their needs. There are now plans to build a jungle spa and a deluxe honeymoon suite. But there are clouds on the horizon as well.

Perhaps more threatening than the number of new businesses opening in the area is the nature of the developments. Flourescent signs, mini marts, massage parlours, bars and internet shops now vie for attention along Khao Sok's roadways.

"I really worry about the type of development," says Art. "Everyone is thinking about business not about nature. I really worry about the music at night, you can hear it three kilometers away. The tourists themselves are responsible," he adds. "If you like to drink and party all night go to Patong. There's a place for that; this is a place for nature."

Art believes that the tourists themselves must help to create a natural experience at Khao Sok, not "just come and see and go away." They should actively encourage the locals to keep the trees, protect the animals,

build appropriate to the setting. "We can make money here only because of the nature," Art says. "If we destroy that, we destroy our livelihoods."

"Some locals are trying to stage full moon parties, beer bars, all the things that draw big crowds in other areas of Thailand, but this has no place in nature."

"The thing in life I enjoy most," says Art, "is to see nature everywhere I go. I'm very happy to sit in the desert, atop a mountain, deep in the jungle ... anywhere in the world as long as there's nature." Art's guests are fortunate that he has created a setting at Khao Sok for them to sit in nature and be equally happy.

PART II
Park Highlights

PARK HIGHLIGHTS

While all national parks have their special attractions, which contributed to their classification as parks in the first place, there are certain inherent dangers in identifying these "highlights". One danger is that visitors will not use their own imagination but flock to these sites (and only these sites) resulting in overuse. Another problem is that the determination of a "special attraction" is such a subjective one. For example, some people will find the night orchestration of frogs along a riverside, or a forest turned to magic by twinkling fireflies to be a highlight of their visit that surpasses the most sublime waterfall.

In Thailand waterfalls hold an almost religious attraction for people and national parks tend to be seen as little more than places to drive to on weekends and holidays for picnics and drinking parties beside the falls. For this reason most national parks in Thailand list anything that even resembles a waterfall as a "park highlight". Khao Sok is no exception to the rule.

The following locations are those officially listed by the National Park Division as Khao Sok's "highlights." But don't feel compelled to see all of these sites and miss the dynamic interactions taking place everywhere else.

It is not uncommon for a group of "gung-ho" hikers to trek 18 kilometers from Park Headquarters to Ton Gloy Waterfall and back but see less wildlife than a weaker member of their party who had to drop out to rest in the first few kilometers. There's an old saying : "It's the sides of the mountain which sustain life – not the summit." When exploring Khao Sok let the journey itself become the destination.

1. MAE YAI WATERFALL
(5.5 km from Park H.Q.)

Thirty five years ago, before the National Park was established, Mae Yai was one of Khao Sok's most remote and spectacular falls with water plunging 100 m through a gorge of lush rainforest. Today it has been reduced to a mere 30 m drop as the construction of Highway 401 between SuratThani and Takuapa has bisected the falls and diverted the water underground through a steel reinforced cement tunnel.

Situated about 5 km from Park Headquarters near the mountain pass to Takuapa, Mae Yai is the only waterfall in Khao Sok National Park that is accessible by car. As one might expect the easy access has not been a blessing to the site. A popular gathering place for teens with booze and boom boxes, Mae Yai has the dubious distinction of being Khao Sok's most littered location.

Though it has little of its former glory and in spite of the abuse, Mae Yai is still very attractive, especially in the rainy season when the flow is at full force. More impressive than the falls, however, is a hike along the highway here. Traffic is still relatively light, the grade is easy for hiking and the views are spectacular. To the east, the forest clad mountains and dramatic karsts that form the southern boundary of the park offer a stunning panorama. On the western side of the mountain pass lush tropical evergreen forest forms a green

HIDDEN TREASURES: *A viewpoint along highway 401 offers a lovely panorama of the Khao Sok valley when approaching from the west 1. Nearby is Mae Yai Waterfall 2. But one must enter the forest itself to discover it's hidden jewels, like the rhinocerous hornbill 3 and the amazing world of insects 4.*

SOK RIVER TRAIL

TON GLOY W.F.

SIP-ET CHAN W.F

⑪
⑩
⑨
⑧
⑫

BANG HUA RAED CREEK

SOK RIVER

BAND JEND RV.

3.5 KM ④
⑥
⑤
②
①
③
⑦

TANG NAM

PARK HEADQUARTERS

SOK RIVER

BRIDGE

WING HIN WATERFALL

TAN SAWAN WF.

FEATURE	DISTANCE (FROM PARK HEADQUARTERS)
1. WING HIN (WATERFALL)	2.8 KM.
2. BANG HUA RAED (CREEK)	3 KM.
3. WANG YAOW (SWIMMING HOLE)	3.3 KM.
4. CAMP SITE & SWIMMING	3.5 KM.
5. CAMP SITE & SWIMMING	4 KM.
6. BANG LE-AP NAM (RAPIDS)	4.5 KM.
7. TAN SAWAN (WATERFALL)	9 KM.
8. TANG NAM (GORGE)	6 KM.
9. LOOKOUT	6.5 KM.
10. BIG TREE TRAIL	8 KM.
11. TON GLOY WATERFALL AND CAMPSITE	9 KM.
12. ENDEMIC SPECIES TRAIL	3.5 KM.

KEY

▨▨▨ ROAD

〰〰 BRIDGE

-------- TRAIL

mantle all the way down to the Takuapa lowlands. At the summit of the pass one can stand at the divide between the Gulf of Thailand and Andaman Sea watersheds. One can even find Nepenthes, the insectiverous pitcher plants, growing along the roadway at this higher elevation.

There are no established forest trails here as yet, but the ridgetops in both directions are major wildlife corridors and staging grounds for the rare Great argus pheasant (Argusianus argus).

2. WING HIN WATERFALL
(2.8 km from Park H.Q.)

Wing Hin is the closest waterfall to the Park Headquarters, but as luck would have it, it's also one of the smallest. The rainy season offers the best display of cataracts here, but in the dry months (December to April) it is usually reduced to little more than a trickle.

Wing Hin is still a lovely place to relax and take in the beauty of the region in an easy half day outing. It is located midway along the Interpretive Trail and makes for a nice rest stop enroute.

To reach Wing Hin follow the main roadway from Park Headquarters to Bang Hua Raed (Rhinocerous Creek). Just a few meters before reaching the creek at the end of the roadway a clearly marked trail leads off to the left. Follow this footpath down to the Sok River where the river runs through a series of huge boulders. This place is called "Bang Win Hin" (rocks where the river runs). You must ford the Sok River at this site to reach Wing Hin which flows from a tributary on the other side. The river crossing can be dangerous in high water and nearly impossible in full flood

so exercise caution. A liana vine is sometimes stretched across the river here for safety in crossing. Wing Hin falls are just out of sight around a bend in this Sok River tributary and many hikers complain that they cannot find them. Use your exploring skills a bit here; it's more fun than too many signs or too troden a path.

Hornbills are frequently seen flying overhead here and in the morning hours gibbons can be heard calling from the canopy. Porcupine, fishing cat, yellow throated marten, otter and monitor lizards all frequent this area, but you will usually need early morning or evening hours and a good deal of luck to see them.

3. BANG HUA RAED WATERFALL
(3 km from Park H.Q.)

Anyone who has viewed the great waterfalls of the world would have trouble classifying these rapids as a waterfall. There are actually two levels where the water is in free fall – one at the confluence of Bang Hua Raed and the Sok River, the other on the Sok River itself – so this site has been listed by the Park Service as "Bang Hua Raed Waterfall". So be it.

Bang Hua Raed (Rhinocerous Creek) is pleasant enough without having to stretch the imagination envisioning waterfalls. Before the road-way was closed to vehicular traffic in 1995 (at the request of conservation-minded Princess Sirindhorn) this site was popular as a drive-in picnic location. Today the parking area is beginning to overgrow and the litter problem has been greatly reduced.

Bang Hua Raed is midway along the Interpretive Trail and marks the end of the roadway and beginning of the

SOK RIVER TRAIL: *Three km. into the trail a foot bridge over Ban Hua Raed 1 leads visitors into primary forest. View of upper Sok River watershed from lookout 2. Big trees 3 & 4 distinguish the trail just before reaching Ton Gloy waterfall 5. Flying lemur 6, are among the many species of mammals inhabiting the Sok River watershed, and binturang 7, the largest member of the civet family, have been seen here.*

more intimate and interesting forest trail to Ton Gloy waterfalls

There's a lot of aquatic life in these waters which a naturalist could spend many hours exploring and probing. Even casual hikers are likely to encounter the red-necked keelback, a beautiful snake, about one meter long, with olive green coloration and a red band near the head. These mildly venomous snakes prey heavily on the frogs singing along the shoreline here. A five-meter Asian reticulated python is also a frequent visitor to Bang Hua Raed.

4. WANG YAOW

(3.3 km from Park H.Q.)

Just a short distance upstream from Bang Hua Raed is a deep water swimming area known as Wang Yaow. There are no waterfalls or rapids here but lovely blue green waters in a wide channel with sandy banks.

Wang Yaow is easily reached via a short side trail that branches off from the main trail to Ton Gloy Waterfall. It is also a station stop for "Nocturnal Animals and Wildlife Tracks" along the Interpretive trail.

If you see fresh wildlife tracks along the shoreline here please try not to disturb them when entering and exiting the river for swimming. Others will enjoy making the same discovery.

5. ENDEMIC SPECIES TRAIL

(3.5 km from Park H.Q.)

This old trail used by tin ore miners more than a decade ago had become overgrown until the discovery of the rafflesia flower here in 1994. It is not often that a new route opens to view a newly discovered endemic species (Rafflesia Kerri Meijer) only to discover another new and endemic species : Palm langkow (Kerriodoxa elegans), the most endangered palm species in the world.

Rafflesia, or *"Bua poot"* as it is locally called, is one of the world's rarest plant species and may be seen at the end of this trail from December to February. Most of the year the plant is little more than microscopic filaments which parasitize a ground-loving liana vine. Small welts begin to form under the liana bark that slowly swell to the size of a soccer ball by December. The flower usually blooms in January – a spectacular 80 cm bloom; it is only slightly smaller than a species of rafflesia restricted to Sumatra which holds the record as the world's largest flower. Within days the great flower begins to wither, blacken and die. Seven buds bloomed here in 1995, only two in 1996. A huge bamboo die-back in 1997 buried the rafflesia site under 3 meters of bamboo and closed much of the upper trail. It is still uncertain if the same site will bloom again.

Just as unique as *"Bua poot"* is Palm langkow, a lovely fan-shaped palm which flourishes along the steep embankments of the trail. This 3-5 m high palm rises from a single thick trunk and displays large round leaves with green upper surfaces and silver-white undersides.The IUCN Red Data Book lists Palm langkow as the world's most endangered palm species. It is found here at Khao Sok, on nearby Khao Phra Taew forest reserve in Phuket, and nowhere else on Earth. Again, do not disturb this plant in any way.

The Endemic Species Trail begins 2 km from Park Headquarters

SIPET CHAN TRAIL : *The TAT forest interpretation trail begins just behind the park visitor center* **1.** *Elevated cement steps and walkways* **2-3** *are designed for heavy visitor use. A Malay pangolin (Scaley anteater)* **4.** *curls into a armour protected ball when frightened. A tremendous diversity of fungi* **5** *thrive in this rainforest watershed. The first of six river crossings along the trail can be a challenge during high water* **6.**

52   *Waterfalls & Gibbon Calls*

along the main road way. It continues from a clearly posted junction another 1.5 km to the rafflesia flower site. The footpath starts out on a gradual gradient through a lovely creek setting where a few huge emergent trees with flared root bases flank the creek. The trail then begins a steep ascent on a hillside where the Palm langkow flourishes. Take your time on the climb to view these unique plants and you won't get too winded.

Stump-tailed macaque, and binturang, the largest member of the civet family which looks like a cross between a bear and a cat, have been spotted along this route. Dusky langurs, lar gibbons and white crowned hornbills are quite common here.

Please do not explore off-trail in this area. It is extremely sensitive habitat for rare and endangered plants we still know little about. It is also downright dangerous : holes dug in the ground by tin ore miners are sometimes extremely deep and a fall could prove fatal.

6. BANG LE-AP NAM WATERFALL
(4.5 km from Park H.Q.)

This is yet another popular swimming area along the Sok River which is accessed via a short side path off the main trail to Ton Gloy Waterfall. Bang Le-ap Nam has no high waterfall but a few chutes in the river where the entire flow is concentrated. Deep emerald green waters enclosed by slickrock and surrounded by lush forest offer the real attractions. A jungle swing fashioned from rattan vine is also popular. Many bird species can be seen in this area especially when the trees are in fruit or flower.

7. TANG NAM GORGE
(6 km from Park H.Q.)

Thais, like many people in the world, flock to waterfalls with almost religious devotion. River canyons, too, can hold a lure of their own, and while it is no Grand Canyon, Tang Nam gorge casts a very special spell.

Here over countless centuries the Sok River has eroded a dramatic gorge through the ancient bedrock and formed a deep pool rich with fish and other aquatic life. The rock walls are festooned in lovely mosses and ferns suspended from many ledges – a most attractive and cool respite from a hard day's hike.

The trail to Tang Nam turns off from the main trail to Ton Gloy about 6km from Park Headquarters. It is clearly posted, but be careful on the steep descent. Wildlife frequently observed in this area includes : several species of kingfishers, otter, fish eagles, water monitors and a wealth of aquatic life.

8. TAN SAWAN WATERFALL
(9 km from park H.Q.)

Tan Sawan is the least visited, but most beautiful waterfall in the Sok River watershed. Here the Bang Jend River falls from a high precipice in bridal veils of white spray before cascading into a deep turquoise pool. Mist suspended in air creates beautiful rainbows when the sun penetrates the dark green canyon in the mid-day hours. It is one of those magical places that is worth every bit the effort to get there.

The approach to Tan Sawan can be difficult, and downright dangerous in the rainy season if the flow is strong. The trail to Tan Sawan branches off from the main trail to Ton Gloy about 5 km from Park Headquarters and winds its way down to the Sok River. One must ford the main river at this point and ascend the Bang Jend tributary to the south. The last 1.5 kilometers to the falls requires wading up this tributary as there is nothing in the way of a trail system.

Even in the dry season fording the Sok River will present a challenge to anyone determined to stay dry. Plan to get very wet on this route. Bring along sneakers or sandals with heel support for the constant river crossings, and good plastic bags for cameras and other valuables.

There is a wonderful swimming area at the base of the falls and considerable wildlife in this remote region of the park. Malay sun bear, tapir, tiger, hornbill, gibbon, langur, wild pig and argus pheasant have been spotted along the ridge tops of this tributary.

Plan a full day for this destination. It's the same distance as Ton Gloy but, without trails, it's far more rugged a trek.

9. TON GLOY WATERFALL
(9 km from Park H.Q.)

Ton Gloy Waterfall is one of Khao Sok's most popular destinations for back country hikers. The first 3 km of the trail follows an old roadway which is also part of the Interpretive Trail system featured in this book. The last 6 km are far more intimate and feature some grand dipterocarp and fig trees, good vistas up the valley and excellent wildlife habitat.

The grade of this route is not difficult but the heat can take its toll when trekking at midday. As the trail follows the course of the Sok River the entire way one is never far from a refreshing dip in a cool river pool. Two km before reaching the falls there is a lovely lookout of the upper valley. The trail then drops down to the river level and winds its way through a grove of stately trees, huge dipterocarps and strangler figs.

Gibbons, langurs, macaques, flying lizards and lemurs, hornbills, jungle fowl, barking deer, and wild boar are often seen along this trail. The site of Ton Gloy falls is a good place to view the great hornbill, especially in the morning and evening hours when the nearby fig trees are in fruit.

The Ton Gloy waterfall is a single level fall that maintains a strong flow all year as the entire Sok River plunges over the precipice in a single chute. With deep forest pools for swimming and smooth slick rock for sunning, Ton Gloy is one of the park's favorite walk-in picnic and camping sites. Please help keep it clean. This is a well-frequented area despite its remoteness; pack out someone else's garbage if necessary.

10. SIP ET CHAN WATERFALL
(4 km from Park H.Q.)

This popular trail begins at a series of stone steps which climb a hill behind the Park's Visitor Information Centre and follows the course of Bang Laen River for 4 km to the base of the falls.

The first part of this trail system has recently become an "interpretive trail" subsidized by the Tourism Authority of Thailand (TAT). Wide as a city sidewalk, the elevated walkway is designed for

SIPET CHAN
WATERFALL TRAIL

FEATURES

1. KHAO SOK N.P. VISITOR & INTERPRETIVE CENTER
2. T.A.T. ELEVATED, NATURE INTERPRETATION TRAIL
3. BAMBOO & SAGO PALM FOREST
4 & 5. HUGE RIVER BANK TREES
6. SIP ET CHAN (ELEVEN TIERED) WATERFALL
7. STEEP RAINFOREST VALLEY (TIGER HABITAT)

KEY

	PAVED ROAD
	DIRT ROAD
	BRIDGE
	TRAIL

BANG LAEN RIVER

TRAIL TO TON GLOY W.F.

SOK RIVER

DIRT ROAD TO BUNGALOWS →

HIGHWAY 401

K.M. 108

Waterfalls & Gibbon Calls 55

FLOODED FORESTS: *Cheow Lan Lake dazzles increasing numbers of visitors with it's extraordinary beauty.*
Dead standing trees in the reservoir pose a hazard to boats, but provide important perches for fish-eating eagles, owls, osprey and kingfishers. Snags also provide mynas, woodpeckers and owls with important nesting cavities.

heavy visitor use, i.e., the tour bus crowd, who prefer their jungle treks in high heels. The tons of steel, reinforced cement, and cable, used to construct this 8.5 million baht walkway will likely become an obstacle course in the future as slopes slip and trees topple across it. For now it offers Khao Sok's only leech-free hiking experience. The English language interpretive signs are largely unintelligible, but don't let this stop you from trying to "interpret" them.

Just as the TAT trail is overbuilt, the trail beyond it to the falls is under-maintained.

The grade is a bit steep at first as the trail climbs a ridge and occassionally dips in and out of ravines. The second half of the trail is considerably easier walking as it follows the course of Bang Laen through a broad, relatively flat floodplain with dense stands of mature bamboo. It is necessary to cross Bang Laen River six times to reach the waterfall and while this can be challenging during full flood (June - October), it is simply a matter of rock hopping in the dry season (December - May). Between the fifth and sixth river crossings there are a number of large emergent trees with huge root bases and massive crowns that afford excellent wildlife viewing opportunities when they are in fruit.

The Sip Et Chan Waterfall, while not large, displays a powerful torrent in the rainy season, and offers a pleasant respite in the dry months with eleven tiers of falls plunging into smooth rock swimming pools. Be careful climbing to the upper level of the falls especially if the rock is wet. There have been many serious accidents around waterfalls in Thailand's national parks.

Lar gibbon songs are usually heard along the trail to Sip Et Chan as is the hysterical call of the rare helmeted hornbill. Leopard, tiger and rare species of pittas are spotted at times while signs of wild pig, barking deer, mouse deer, Malay sunbear and scaley anteater are very common.

11. CHEOW LAN LAKE

While the construction of Rachabrapah Dam in 1982 by the Electricity Generating Authority of Thailand (EGAT) was an unmitigated disaster for the park's wildlife, it created a vast lake – Cheow Lan – that is the premier showpiece of Khao Sok National Park. Huge limestone outcrops, known as karsts, rise here directly from the lake edge to elevations up to 960 meters – more than three times the height of karsts in world famous Halong Bay or Phangnga Bay. This stunning landscape is still one of Thailand's best kept secrets. Phangnga Bay, for instance, gets more visitors in a single week than Cheow Lan Lake receives in an entire year.

The Rachabrapah Dam, located 65 km from the Park Headquarters on a well marked spur road from highway 401, provides the only road access to the lake. A security card is necessary to enter the EGAT generating site. From here boats can be rented from either the National Park Substation 2 or from local fishermen to tour the lake.

Canoes and kayaks are becoming more and more popular ways to view this magnificent setting, though there are few currently available to rent. One could spend weeks in this 165 square km lake exploring its many long arms, hidden coves, creeks and grottos.

The park maintains four floating

CAVES TRAIL: *1 Tone Teuy is the staging area for hikers bound for Seeroo, Namtaloo and Kangkow caves. 2 A "jungle jacuzzi" half way along the trail to Namtaloo is perfect for a refreshing dip. 3 Namtaloo Cave entrance passage. 4 A softshell, snapping turtle found in Tone Teuy Creek 5. Much of the trail follows the pristine creek course along active wild elephant trails 6. 7 A boat disembarks passengers at the trail head.*

lodges on the lake for overnight visitor use. The vertical nature of much of the shoreline precludes camping in most areas and fires in this area are always of concern.

Wildlife most frequently seen along the shores of the lake during the day are: gibbons (especially in the early hours of the day when they call), langurs, macaques, osprey, eagles, and several species of hornbill. Also commonly sighted or heard are: barking deer, otter, monitor lizard, red jungle fowl, greater coucals, great argus pheasants, Chinese pond herons and wild pig. Asian elephants occassionally swim out to some of the lake's 100 islands to forage on bamboo, but this is a rare sight indeed. Both elephant and tiger frequent the shores near the smaller floating lodge – Tone Teuy (Substation 4).

12. CAVES & LAKE TRAIL

An increasingly popular access route to Cheow Lan Lake is to bypass the Rachabrapah Dam site altogether and hike in from Highway 401 (the Surat Thani - Takuapa road) along an old logging road. A park ranger is required to accompany hiking parties on this route as it is prime habitat for wild elephant. More than one tourist has been challenged by cow elephants protecting young calves.

The route is rapidly overgrowing and now resembles a trail more than a logging road. Banks are eroding along some sidecast slopes and bridges over creeks have rotted away with the passage of time, but the grade is good for a relatively easy 7-12 km trek.

Look for an old road bed heading up the hillside to the north of Highway 401 close to KM 99. From here the trail climbs gradually to a low pass then descends down to the end of a long arm of the lake. It is possible to reach one arm of the lake after hiking only 7 km but you will need a pre-arranged boat pick-up at this point. The longer route of 12 km takes one to a small falls in Tone Teuy Creek where it enters Cheow Lan lake. From here it is a very short boat ride (or swim) to Substation 4 raft house.

Tone Teuy Creek is also the starting point for reaching three fascinating caves within 4-6 km of Substation 4 raft house. From the raft house the route to the caves involves wading up Tone Teuy Creek a considerable distance before embarking on an elephant path through large grazing areas and primary forest. There was a lot of disturbance in this area during the "communist" era as areas were cleared for rice cultivation. Today, however, this trail system is used by wildlife as much as humans. Elephant dung, crater - like footprints and ravaged feeding areas give testimony to its use. Tiger, serow, barking deer, bear, pig-tail and stump-tailed macaques, wild boar and other signs of wildlife are abundant.

Namtaloo cave is located approx. 6 km. from the Substation 4 raft house. The route to this cave passes a garden of water-eroded limestone outcrops which lend a hauntingly beautiful backdrop to the lush forest. Just before reaching the cave one passes a few dug-out bunker installations made by communist insurgents between 1975-1982. The entrance to Namtaloo is distinguished by a huge fang-like stalactite. What is more disconcerting is the sudden

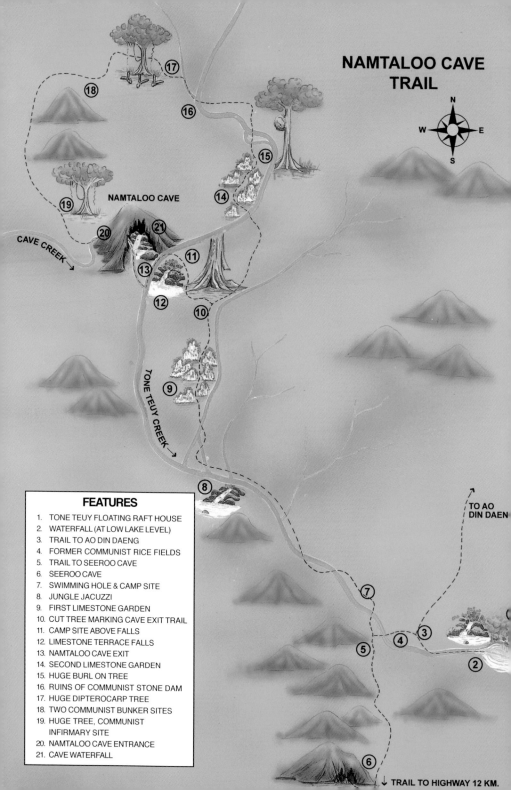

NAMTALOO CAVE TRAIL

NAMTALOO CAVE

CAVE CREEK

TONE TEUY CREEK

TO AO
DIN DAEN

FEATURES

1. TONE TEUY FLOATING RAFT HOUSE
2. WATERFALL (AT LOW LAKE LEVEL)
3. TRAIL TO AO DIN DAENG
4. FORMER COMMUNIST RICE FIELDS
5. TRAIL TO SEEROO CAVE
6. SEEROO CAVE
7. SWIMMING HOLE & CAMP SITE
8. JUNGLE JACUZZI
9. FIRST LIMESTONE GARDEN
10. CUT TREE MARKING CAVE EXIT TRAIL
11. CAMP SITE ABOVE FALLS
12. LIMESTONE TERRACE FALLS
13. NAMTALOO CAVE EXIT
14. SECOND LIMESTONE GARDEN
15. HUGE BURL ON TREE
16. RUINS OF COMMUNIST STONE DAM
17. HUGE DIPTEROCARP TREE
18. TWO COMMUNIST BUNKER SITES
19. HUGE TREE, COMMUNIST
    INFIRMARY SITE
20. NAMTALOO CAVE ENTRANCE
21. CAVE WATERFALL

↓ TRAIL TO HIGHWAY 12 KM.

realization that the creek one has been following upstream for 6 km. now appears to reverse direction, flowing into the cave rather than out of it. It's a different creek.

Namtaloo is a classic, river-eroded cave 10-15 m. wide and more than 500 m long. It features pristine cave formations, columns, stalagmites, stalactites, calcite ponds and rimstone flow formations. The river which flows through the cave year round is rich in cave aquatic life. Some of the cave dwellers one might encounter include : cave crickets, cave toad, hunter spider, scorpion spider, a variety of bat species and the Malayan stripe-tailed racer, with it's creamy colored body and black and white striped tail.This amazing snake lives in total darkness and climbs sheer cave walls in search of slumbering bats which it seizes and swallows. Tracks of tiger, elephant and other large mammals are often seen along the creek banks near the cave entrance.

"Kangkow" or Bat Cave is reached via a narrow cliff ledge where caution must be exercised. The humid, smelly vault is rich in bat guano and overhead, hanging in the gloomy darkness, are thousands of bats. Please do not disturb them with bright light– they need their rest for the important work they do. "Seeroo Cave" only 4 km from Namtaloo Cave, has become a bit of a mecca for history buffs. Here communist insurgents (a euphemism for students disillusioned with their government), were able to hold off the Thai army for seven years between 1975 and 1982. Seeroo Cave has four passageways which converge into one great chamber. Until quite recently remnants of the relatively recent communist occupation of the site could be found in empty shell casings and old food containers. Elephants now use these passageways, as their footprints reveal, and it is hard to imagine this serene setting ever being the site of bloody conflict. (See "Profiles" pg.34). Check yourself carefully for ticks after a dry season visit to this cave.

BAT HABITS: *Not all bats live in caves. Insectivorous bats (top) rely on sonar to find their prey in the dark and navigate cave chambers. Fruit-eating bats (bottom) rely instead on night vision and a keen sense of smell to find their food; they roost hanging from trees.*

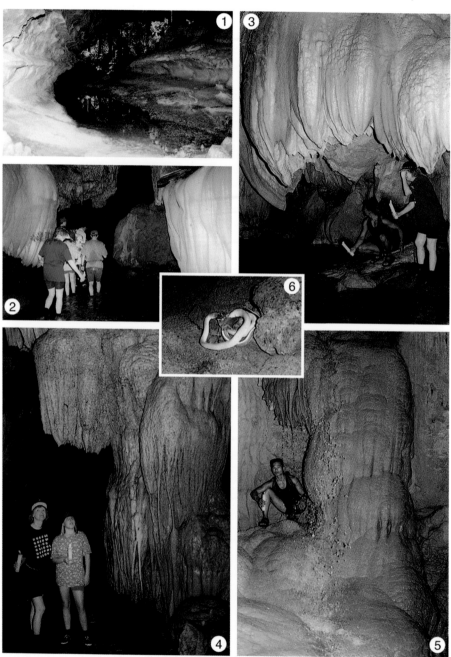

NAMTALOO – A RIVER RUNS THROUGH IT: *Namtaloo's river eroded entrance 1 leads to spectacular flow formations 2, 3 and 4, and a surprise waterfall 5 located midway through the cave passage. Cave life is rich and varied. A Striped tailed cave racer 6 is seen here crushing and swallowing a living bat.*

WARNING: Namtaloo Cave Adventure
Live to Tell About It !

"One minute I was in what I thought was the most beautiful place in the world. The next thing there was death all around me." These are the words of 21-year old Helena Carrol, the sole survivor of a disaster in Namtaloo Cave that claimed eight lives in October 2007.

A party of seven tourists with two inexperienced guides had made the fatal mistake of trying to traverse Namtaloo's 500 m long cave passage during the height of the rainy season. In the shelter of the cave, and during the hour or more it takes to traverse it, there was no way of knowing that heavy rains in the surrounding forest outside the cave were swelling the river.

Helena said the party heard a roar behind them when she and her fiancé quickly climbed up onto some high ledges in the narrowest part of the cave while the flash flood washed away the rest of the group. Fearing they too would die if he did not go for help, her fiancé reentered the water where he too perished. The young girl spent the rest of the day and night in the total dark of the cave, staring at glow-worms, until she was rescued the following day.

Helena's party was not the first fatalities at Namtaloo. A few years earlier another young woman ignored the advice of her guide and insisted on completing the cave passage even though the water level was rapidly rising. She too perished. Don't become the next victim.

The Namtaloo Cave passage is probably the greatest adventure Khao Sok has to offer, but it would be remiss for this book not to bring these tragedies to public attention. Here are some rules for entering the cave that might save your life.

1) Do not attempt to traverse Namtaloo Cave in the rainy season or if there is the threat of rain at any time of year. It is normally safe to enter the large chambers near the entrance, but beware once the cave passage starts to constrict. This is the danger zone. Returning back the way you entered will make your hike longer, but it will also ensure your safety.

2) Make certain your guides are experienced and do not try to over rule them if they say it is too dangerous to do the traverse.

3) Allow at least 20-30 minutes between hiking groups and do not try to overtake another party already in the cave. It is confusing enough for guides to keep track of their group in the dark without compounding the situation.

4) Only hike in one direction, following the flow of the stream. A bottleneck of hikers at the narrowest part of the cave greatly increases the time for passage for both parties and puts them at greater risk of being caught in a flash flood.

5) Do not pass through the cave with water bottles in hand. You will need both hands free to work your way over ledges and through deep water. Let your guide carry your water. Headlamps are also better than hand-held torches.

6) If your guide ignore these safety procedures, tell them their services are terminated and report them to park authorities. Your life may depend on it.

KHAO SOK NATIONAL PARK
TRAIL ETIQUETTE

With increasing visitor use Khao Sok National Park needs everyone's help to protect the very special values here. Please do your part by reading and observing these few basic rules:

1.) Please do not dispose of any litter along the trails or camping sites. This includes: plastic water bottles, snack food wrappings, film packaging and cigarette butts. Trash receptacles are available for litter at the Park Headquarters and other sites throughout the Park tourist zone.
   Note: It is now illegal to take styrofoam lunch containers into national parks. Biodegradeable Ku-Green products are available at the park visitors center.

2.) There are no toilet facilities along Park trails. Please be considerate of others. Never defecate within 20 meters of a stream, river or trail. Water supplies risk serious contamination by carelessness. Dig a shallow hole with a stick or trowel, burn your toilet paper, and completely bury your waste with soil so that if someone were to step on that spot they would never know that site was used. Women please, do not leave toilet paper lying on the ground after urinating (always burn or bury it, or carry it out in a trash bag). Tampons and pads must be carried out in plastic bags with litter and garbage.

3.) Use only biodegradable soaps when washing in the streams and rivers. Never dump phosphate detergents into the river when washing clothes. Use a basin for washing and pour detergent water into a small pit dug some distance away from the water course. Khao Sok National Park still has pristine aquatic ecosystems. Let's keep them that way.

4.) Use only dead driftwood for fires and aways be sure that cooking fires are kept small, built on sand or mineral soil, and that they are completely extinguished before leaving your campsite. Do not leave half-burnt trash: cans, plastic, etc. in your fire pit. Always carry it out with you.

5.) Please practice "no trace" camping. Pretend that you and your party are being pursued and take caution when leaving your campsite that the following group can find no trace of you having been there.

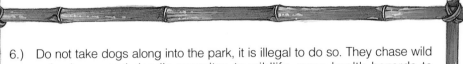

6.) Do not take dogs along into the park, it is illegal to do so. They chase wild animals, spread deadly parasites to wildlife, pose health hazards to humans, and greatly reduce your chances of viewing wild animals.

7.) Do not drive motorcycles, jeeps on other vehicles along Park trail systems. It is extremely disruptive to wildlife and hiking parties. It is also illegal and you will be fined.

8.) Please keep noise levels and smoking to a minimum along the trails – both greatly decrease your chances of wildlife viewing and can be disruptive to other parties.

9.) Do not aftempt to feed, harm, or harass wild animals, Always keep camp food out of their reach. Khao Sok's wildlife is still extremely shy but with increasing visitor use macaque monkeys, bears, jungle rats and other animals could become a nuisance as a result of human misbehavior.

10.) If you see anyone hunting or poaching Park wildlife, destroying or stealing plants, please report to Park Headquarters, and send a letter to head office in Bangkok (address, page 70)

11.) Please be respectful of Thai culture and tradition and do not bathe nude at the waterfalls.

12.) Do not touch cave formations; oil from your fingers will blacken the calcium carbonate. Never carve or paint initials on cave walls and refrain from toilet use inside cave chambers and passages.

13.) Do not discard water bottles or cigarette butts in the cave. Smoking is noxious for slumbering bats; don't do it.

14.) Obey your guide if he says the water level is too dangerous for passage through Namtaloo Cave. Allow 20-30 minutes between groups and never try to overtake another party in the dark. Hike one way-downstream only-and stay to the streambed. Walking along the cave floor removes the fungus growing atop the bat guano that cave crickets depend upon.

REMEMBER

The best guarantee that Khao Sok National Park will be as wild and wonderful for future generations as it is for you, is your behavior today.

**KLONG
NAKHA
WILDLIFE
SANCTUARY**

KLONG
NAKHA
WILDLIFE
SANCTUARY

KLONG
SAENG
WILDLIFE
SANCTUARY

KHAO SOK
NATIONAL PARK

KLONG PHANOM
NATIONAL PARK

20

24

25

30

23

18

17　14

16

13　19

15

9　10

12

7　3　5

8　6　4　2

1　11

KM
99

**SRI
PHANG NGA
NATIONAL PARK**

TO TAKUAPA & PHUKET

KM
108

401

**KLONG
PHANOM
NATIONAL PARK**

LONG
AENG
WILDLIFE
SANCTUARY

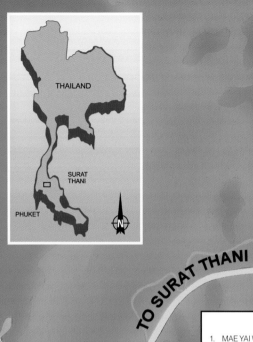

THAILAND

SURAT
THANI

PHUKET

N

TO SURAT THANI

22

21

401

TO KRABI

PHUKET

FEATURE

1. MAE YAI W.F.
2. WING HIN W.F.
3. BANG HUA RAED W.F.
4. WANG YAOW
5. PARK VISITOR CENTER
6. BANG LE-AP NAM W.F.
7. TAN NAM GORGE
8. TAN SAWAN W.F.
9. TON GLOY W.F.
10. SIP ET CHAN W.F.
11. PANTOORAT MTN.
12. KLONG KA RAFT HOUSE
13. CAVE & LAKE TRAIL
14. TONE TEUY RAFT HOUSE
15. NANG PRY RAFT HOUSE
16. SEROO CAVE
17. NAMTALOO CAVE
18. KANGKOW CAVE
19. HIGHEST MTN. IN PARK-KHAO SEROW
20. KRAISON FLOATING RAFT HOUSE
21. RACHABRAPAH DAM & BOAT PIER
22. NATIONAL PARK PIER
23. FLYING FOX COLONY
24. VIEW POINT TRAIL
25. CHEOW LAN TOUR RAFT HOUSE
26. PLERN PRAI RAFT HOUSE
27. SAI CHOI RAFT HOUSE
28. THALE NAI RAFT HOUSE
29. PAKARANG CAVE
30. TREE TOPS JUNGLE SAFARI RAFT HOUSE

KEY

▨▨▨▨	PAVED ROAD
- - - -	DIRT ROAD
═══	BRIDGE
- - - - -	TRAIL

PART III
Visitors Guide

PARK FACILITIES

There are four park-operated bungalows beside the Khao Sok Park Headquarters which can accommodate up to 33 people and a camping area for larger groups. A small restaurant and concession stand is operated within the park near the picnic area beside Bang Laen River. A Visitor Information Centre has good informative displays on the park in both English and Thai, and one can secure maps here as well as browse through a small nature library.

Park accommodation is also provided at Cheow Lan Lake Substation 2 for up to 18 people in bungalows overlooking the lake. Much more popular are the floating raft houses. The oldest raft house, Nang Pry (Substation 3) can accommodate up to 50 people in comfortable units with 2-3 beds per room, hardwood floors, screened windows and built-in shower / toilets. Unfortunately, the toilet facilites, (molded fiberglass units designed for tiny Japanese apartments) not only look incongruous but empty directly into the lake. This raft house location is dramatic in terms of scenery as the limestone karsts in this region of the lake are truly spectacular.

Tone Teuy (Substation 4) raft house accommodates people in a much more primitive style. It has 12 very small bamboo huts with floor mattresses and communal toilet facilities located down a long wobbly walkway. The feeling here is more isolated, though less dramatic. It is a lovely green arm of the lake, very near the trail to the caves and popular with adventure tour groups. A third floating raft house, Kraison, has 9 raft houses, a large floating *sala* for overflow, as well as several large group rooms built on the hillside. Sunrises from here are often spectacular.

Klong Ka is the newest park facility on the lake. It can sleep 72 people in 6 large group units, all with private toilets. The views from the hillside restaurant and lodges is stunning, but the stairway access is very steep and the area seems prone to landslides. Advanced bookings at all park accomodations are recommended in the high season (November to April) to avoid disappointment.

The nearest town to Khao Sok is Takuapa, 40 km. west of Park Headquarters on Highway 401. Hospital, medical clinics, currency exchange, post office, overseas calls, hotel, restaurants and markets are all located here. Local buses run hourly and the trip takes only 30-45 minutes. A timetable for buses is posted at the park's Visitor Centre.

For Reservation and Information contact:
- **Khao Sok National Park.**
  Mailbox 118, Mueang district, Suratthani, 84000
  Tel: 0 7739 5025 or
- **National Park Office**
  National Park, Wildlife and Plant Conservation Department
  61 Phahonyothin rd., Chatuchak, Bangkok 10900
  Tel: 6602579 7223. 66 2561 2919 and 66 2561 4292 Ext. 714, 725
  Room reservation can be made through internet at www.dnp.go.th

PARK SERVICES: *Khao Sok National Park provides a great range of visitor services. The Visitor Center 1 is the first place to stop for an excellent interpretive display, gift shop, and to purchase biodegradeable (potatoe starch edible) lunch containers from very friendly park staff 2. Park vistor facilities include four floating raft houses like Kraisorn 3,4,5, and the newly built Klong Ka facility, built dramatically on a hillside 6 with imposing views 7.*

PRIVATE FACILITIES

In the past decade there has been an explosion of development at Khao Sok; almost every former farmer and fisherman family is now running some type of bungalow business. On the western edge of the park there are now dozens of privately owned lodges catering to guests. Six floating raft houses have opened on a northern arm of Cheow Lan Reservoir to compete with the four raft house complexes operated by the national park.

These facilities vary greatly in architectural style, location and service. Unlike some guide books that judge and rate services, this book will restrict itself to listing them and let you form your own opinions.

Most of the operations that have sprung up along the park boundaries are small family-run businesses. Accommodations range from dramatic cliff side lodges to bare basic bamboo huts. Some of the privately operated bungalows offer tree houses that are the most popular for those wanting to act out their Tarzan and Jane fantasies.

All of the private lodges in operation as this book goes to press are listed here (in no particular order). Their locations correspond with the numbers on the map for Khao Sok Visitor Services, page 73-74.

PLENTY OF ROOM: *Private facilities at Khao Sok to meet the growing tourist demand include six new privately owned raft houses on Cheow Lan Lake, like Sai Choi* **1**, *and thirty-seven lodges on the western end of the park. Smiley Bungalow* **2** *has elevated units, while Baan Khao Sok Resort boasts riverside bungalows and an amazing rain vine restaurant* **3**.

VISITOR SERVICES DIRECTORY

NO	Lodge	Total # of Rooms	Tree Houses	Setting	Phone / e-mail / website
1	Khao Sok Cheewalei		5	Orchard	089-2018994, 081-4960171
2	Worapoj Resort & Gym	5		Riverside / Garden	(66) 087-8887079, (66) 087-8841762 www.worapojresort.com
3	Treetops Jungle Safari		15	Forest / Orchard	084-8458774 www.treetopsjunglesafaris.com
4	Khao Sok Nature Resort	13	11	Forest / Orchard / Riverside	086-1200588, 086 276 9805 natureresort@gmail.com www.tashihandmade.com/nature
5	Khao Sok Riverside Cottage	32		Riverside / Forest	077-395159 khao_sok@hotmail.com
6	Our Jungle House	8	8	Orchard / Garden	081-4170546 ourjunglehouse1985@gmail.com www.khaosokcommodation.com
7	Palm Garden Resort	6		Orchard	077-395002, 085-7850539, 087-2688557
8	Khao Sok Evergreen House	6		Orchard	khaosokevergreenhouse@ khaosokevergreenhouse.net www.khaosokevergreenhouse.net
9	Khao Sok Valley E' Spa	10		Orchard	086-28399233 khaosok@hotmail.com www.khaosokvalleylodge.com
10	Art's Riverview Lodge	15	10	Orchard	087-8856185 www.khaosokart'riverviewlodge.com
11	Bann Khao Sok Resort	7	3	Orchard	081-8945440, 081-9580185 bankhaosok@yahoo.com www.khaosok-accommodation.com
12	Khao Sok Valley Lodge	10	10	Orchard	086-28399233 khaosok@hotmailc.om www.khaosokvalleylodge.com
13	Khao Sok Island Resort	9	9 elevated	Orchard	086-1209476 info@khaosokisland.com www.khaosokisland.com
14	Nung House	18		Orchard	077-395147 nanghouse02@yahoo.com
15	Bamboo House	11	6	Orchard	bamboo_khaosok@hotmail.com www.kribidir.com / bamboo / indek
16	Khao Sok Green Valley Resort	8		Orchard	077-395145, 084-8457916 kraisak@hotmail.com www.khaosokgreenvalley.com
17	Treetops River Huts	29	3	Riverside / Forest Orchard	086-2775268, 077-395143 www.treetops-riverhuts.com
18	Khao Sok Rainforest Resort	21	5	Riverside / Forest Orchard / Garden	077-395135, 077-395136 081-2708282, 089-8276230 khaosokrainforestresort@yahoo.com

VISITOR SERVICES DIRECTORY (Continued)

NO	Lodge	Total # of Rooms	Tree Houses	Setting	Phone / e-mail / website
19	Thanyamundra Organic Resort	9		Riverside / Forest / Orchard	info@thanyamundra.com www.thanyamundra.com
20	Khao Sok River Lodge	12		Riverside / Forest	treking@phuket.ksc.co.th
21	Baan Rim Nam Resort	12		Riverside / Orchard	077-395140, 087-2642340 baanrimnamresort@yahoo.com
22	Morning Mist Resort			Orchard / Garden	089-9718794 www.morningmistresort.com
23	Khao Sok Green View Resort	7		Orchard	087-2632481
24	Khao Sok Jugle Huts	21	1	Riverside / Orchard	087-2646032, 007-395017 www.krabidir.com-khaosokjungles.
25	Smiley Bungalow	20	1	Orchard	077-395156, 089-8715744 smileyland@hotmail.com
26	AT Mountain Resort	10		Orchard	082-1799992, 077-395005 khaowang.2010@gmail.com www.khaosok-athome.com
27	Khao Sok Las Orquides Resort				
28	Khao Banana Hut	6		Orchard	077-395023, 087-0487657 khaosok_eco@hotmail.com
29	Garden Huts	6	6	Orchard	077-375184, 078-810723 tangmo2004@hotmail.com
30	Khao Sok Treehouse Resort		19	Orchard	089-9703353, 089-5906147 khaosok_treehouse@yahoo.com www.khaosok-treehouse.com
31	Thansawan Resort	8		Orchard	077-395150, 082-8075017 yaowapa-m@hotmail.com
32	Cliff And River	25		Riverside / Orchard	www.thecliffand.com

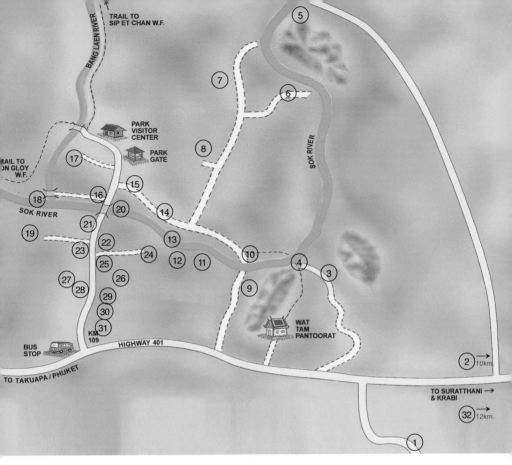

SERVICE DIRECTORY MAP

1. Khao Sok Cheewalei
2. Worapoj Resort & Gym
3. Treetops Jungle Safari
4. Nature Resort
5. Khao Sok Riverside Cottage
6. Our Jungle House
7. Palm View Resort
8. Khao Sok Evergreen House
9. Khao Sok Valley E' Spa
10. Art's Riverview Lodge
11. Baan Khao Sok Resort
12. Khao Sok Valley Lodge
13. Khao Sok Island Resort
14. Nang House
15. Bamboo House
16. Khao Sok Green Valley Resort
17. Treetops River Huts

18. Khao Sok Rainforest Resort
19. Thanyamundra Organic Resort
20. Khao Sok River Lodge
21. Bann Rim Nam Resort
22. Morning Mist Resort
23. Khao Sok Green View Resort
24. Khao Sok Jungle Huts
25. Smiley Bungalow
26. AT Mountain Resort
27. Khao Sok Las Orguideas Resort
28. Khao Banana Hut
29. Khao Sok Paradise Resort
30. Khao Sok Treehouse Resort
31. Thanswan Resort
32. Cliff & River Resort

KEY	
—————	PAVED ROAD
----------	DIRT ROAD
⪢⪡	BRIDGE
············	TRAIL

It seems an inevitable progression in Thailand that a destination put on the map and made popular by budget backpackers will attract and often be replaced by high-end tourism. Well, Khao Sok has come of age. As the first five-star resort makes its way to Khao Sok it is refreshing to see that this venture is not a typical high-rise hotel chain catering to mass tourism. The Thanyamunda Organic Resort, in fact, represents a paradigm shift on tourism.

First and foremost it is an organic farm that combines ancient traditions with experimentation to produce its own fertilizers and natural insecticides for its extensive gardens. The rice, corn, cucumbers, lettuce, pole beans, Chinese cabbage, eggplant, and other organic crops produced here are used to serve deliciously fresh and healthy meals not only to resort guests, but to feed students at the new Phuket International Academy and its adjacent four star Thanyachiva Lifestyle Resort. Thailand's newest hospitality group launched all three projects simultaneously.

The brainchild of a visionary entrepreneur, who prefers quiet anonymity to fame, Thanyamundra describes itself as "a boutique, sustainable 5 star organic resort offering sanctuary, dedicated to the ultimate private rejuvenation of body, mind and soul in the most natural yet sophisticated personalized form." It's quite a claim, but any visitor to the site will quickly realize it's also more than the usual hype.

First and foremost there is the setting. In a world where location is everything – Thanyamundra has it! Located in the heart of Khao Sok's bungalow belt, the road that leads from the highway to the park headquarters, a passerby would hardly know that Thanyamundra's sprawling 75-rai estates is even there. A wall of living bamboo and a private entrance gate only hints that something special lies beyond. Three years ago this property was an overgrown hillside of scrub forest and abandoned orchards. No one saw it as a building site for bungalows much less a resort, but careful clearing and grooming revealed a surprising oasis of nature, serenity and seclusion.

From the 50 meter long infinity pool that now sits atop the highest point of the property as well as the luxurious teakwood villas that grace the hillside sloping down to the Sok River, pampered guests can look across to the tropical forested hills of Khao Sok National Park and all the way down the mist-shrouded Sok River Valley to the looming karsts that surround Cheow Lan lake. If any setting at Khao Sok has the ability to lift the spirit, it is surely here. With gibbons singing their morning duets from the nearby forest and songbirds darting about the grounds with their cheery chirps, breakfast served in the open-air verandah becomes as much a symphony of nature as a visual and culinary feast for the mind, body and soul.

Guest at Thanyapundra have opportunities at their doorstep to indulge the senses with massage, calm the mind with meditation, explore trails that lead directly into the park or get delightfully dirty helping to plant and harvest crops from the extensive organic gardens. There are few places in Thailand where tourists can connect so closely with the natural environment, themselves and their food. The resort owners hope that this agro tourism venture will inspire farmers throughout the Sok River Valley to shift from the toxic herbicides, pesticides and insecticides that now contaminate the soil and river of the region to more organic and sustainable farming practices. That prospect alone makes Thanyamundra a most welcome addition to the neighborhood.

LODGE SIGHTINGS: *With a little luck, visitors to Khao Sok may view wildlife near their bungalow. Treehouses 1 are good for bird viewing and seeing noctural animals like Barking deer 2 far below on the forest floor, or the nocturnal Slow loris 3 feeding on insects in the tree branches, Long tail macaques 4 are commonly sighted, as are several species of playful otters 5. The Ruddy kingfisher 6 is one of several spectacular kingfishers found at Khao Sok near the river.*

GETTING THERE

Khao Sok National Park is situated in south Thailand just below the Isthmus of Kra – the narrowest neck of the Malay peninsula. The nearest international airport is Phuket, located 170 km from Park Headquarters. Surat Thani, only 120 km from the park, has daily flight connections with Bangkok.

Highway 401, connecting SuratThani and Takuapa offers the only public road access to the park. Air-con bus service from Phuket and Surat Thani are available every hour from 7:30 am to noon, while local buses run approximately every hour from dawn to 3.30 pm. There is now direct mini van service to Khao Sok from Krabi. To go from Krabi on your own take a local or air con bus bound for Surat Thani and change to the Takuapa bound bus at Phanom junction, get off at km 109.

Kilometer 109 is the jump off point for all buses. Don't worry about counting kilometer markers, just say "Khao Sok" as all the buses are used to visitors embarking and disembarking here. From the highway a 1.5 km side road leads to Park Headquarters and most of the areas lodges. There are usually many enterprising bungalow operators waiting at the bus stop with trucks to solicit guests. Motorcycle taxis can also be arranged here. If you're not going to the bungalow of your pick-up driver just state your destination. There should be no fee and no hassle; the driver gets a commission from the lodge operator where they drop you off.

Taxi service by car and air con mini van is available from Phuket and Surat Thani to Khao Sok. Tuktuk drivers from Takuapa bus station are also easy to hire.

Many people choose to rent a jeep for a few days to explore the countryside enroute to the park. While this is a good way to reach the park and the lake on your own schedule don't plan on 4 wheel driving your way thru the rivers and forest like some Phuket tour company brochures promote. As of 1995 all access into the park proper is closed to vehicles (motorcycles included) and stiff fines are levied on violators. Khao Sok is being managed as a wilderness park so please respect the park and the law.

Rachabrapah Dam, Cheow Lan Lake and the park's floating raft houses are all accessed from a well marked turnoff from Highway 401 at Ban Takum, a small roadside settlement between km 52 and km 53. It is a 14 km journey from the junction to Cheow Lan Lake and Substation 2, Khao Sok National Park.

SUGGESTED KHAO SOK ITINERARY
(I -8 DAYS)

DAY 1 Check in at one of 37 lodges near Park Headquarters.
Orientation at Park Visitor Center.
Hike TAT Interpretive Trail, and if energetic, carry on to Sipet
Chan Waterfall.

DAY 2 Early rise, dawn breakfast, and set off with picnic lunch on
Sok River Trail, using the Interpretive Trail markers for this book.
Choose waterfall site according to ones ability (3-9 km from
Park Headquarters).
Return to lodge late afternoon for relaxing swim, or river tubing.

DAY 3 Morning elephant trek, or birding.
Afternoon canoeing, or tubing down the Sok River.

DAY 4 Consider a day just to relax in a hammock, or on the verandah
of your lodge, to let the serenity of Khao Sok sink in.
Alternately, make your own tour of the many lodges (map, page 82)
to sample the ambience and different menus at each location.

DAY 5 Transfer to Cheow Lan Lake.
Boat to one of 3 floating raft houses (wildlife viewing enroute).
Enjoy lunch, a refreshing swim, or a short hike to Seroo Cave,
Night safari by boat.

DAY 6 Dawn safari by boat.
Hike to Namtaloo Cave and all the way through the passage.
Return to floating raft house for relaxing late afternoon.

DAY 7 Packing a picnic lunch, take a full day to explore Cheow Lan
Lake's hidden and remote reaches.
Consider overnight adventure camp out, or return to floating
rafthouse.

DAY 8 Hike out of Cheow Lan Lake back to highway through prime
elephant habitat, or return journey by boat.

ADVENTURE LAND: *Khao Sok National Park offers visitors a wild range of "soft" adventure from jungle safari by elephants 1, to lake paddling 2, from rock climbing, river rafting, tubing and canoeing, to long treks, interpretive trails and casual hikes.*

WHEN TO GO

The best time to visit Khao Sok National Park is really determined by the type of experience one is looking for. The dry season (December to May) is frequently cited as the best time to go as it is unlikely you will experience much rain at this time of year. The trails are dry, there are far fewer leeches and the river levels are at their lowest making river crossings much easier and camping along riverbanks all the more pleasant.

The down side of the dry season is that the low water levels reduce the volume and majesty of the waterfalls and restrict river navigability for canoeing. There are also far more visitors at this time of year and larger mammals tend to shy further away from the trails. While the dry season has fewer leeches it is the peak season for ticks.

Many long-time residents and repeat visitors to Khao Sok National Park actually prefer the wet season (June to November). After all, what better way to see the rainforest than in the rain. This is the dynamic season when tropical storms dump huge volumes of water in short periods. Rivers turn to raging torrents, huge boulders grate and grind as they are driven downstream, and waterfalls explode in a fury of white water that humbles the few hardy explorers that work their way to these sites.

This is the season when the wild elephants and tiger return from the lake shore to frequent the main trail system of the Sok River watershed. It is also the fruiting season when the orchards in the Khao Sok community are heavy with delicious tropical fruits: rambutan, longon, durian, mango, mangostene, jackfruit and others. It is possible during the rainy season to see park wildlife like Malay and Asiatic black bear, civets, slow loris, wild boar and deer come into the plantations to gorge on the bounty of fruit.

Leeches are perhaps the greatest nuisance of the rainy season. Rain tends to come in heavy downpours for an hour or two each day and there is usually intermittent sunny periods. A poncho and an umbrella come in very handy, and most people prefer these to rain gear which gets stifling hot and humid.

If visitors to Khao Sok are coming for a specific attraction then timing can be critical. Rafflesia only blooms December to February with individual blossoms only lasting 2-3 days before deteriorating. Hornbills begin nesting in January so all of the mated females will be locked up in tree chambers for 2-3 months. Consequently, there will be more hornbills in flight at any other time of year. If, however, you want to see or photograph nesting behavior, this is the only time to come.

For the first time visitor, don't let any season deter you as each has its special features. Khao Sok National Park can cast its spell in any weather and at any time of year.

WHAT TO BRING

DAY HIKE :

- [ ] 2-3 liters of drinking water
- [ ] light snacks, fruit, or sack lunch

- [ ] t-shirt or short sleeve shirt
- [ ] shorts or trousers
- [ ] light weight hiking boots or runners
- [ ] rubber sandals (with heel support) for river crossings
- [ ] umbrella or rain gear (in rainy season)
- [ ] hat

- [ ] sunscreen
- [ ] rub-on insect repellent or tobacco (in socks) for leeches
- [ ] swim suit (nude bathing prohibited)
- [ ] binoculars
- [ ] camera & film
- [ ] small first aid kit

- [ ] toilet paper
- [ ] plastic bag for litter and used toilet paper

Additional Equipment for OVERNITE CAMPING:

- [ ] matches or lighter
- [ ] water purification tablets
- [ ] pocket knife

- [ ] food
- [ ] cooking utensils
- [ ] tent or mosquito net
- [ ] sleeping pad

- [ ] tarp (in rainy season)
- [ ] blanket
- [ ] sweat shirt or light sweater (for cool nights)
- [ ] long trousers
- [ ] biodegradeable soap & shampoo
- [ ] overnite toilet kit

(Remember : Keep it light; it's a hot hike.)

HEALTH & SAFETY TIPS

People commonly associate visits to tropical forests with many hidden dangers: tigers that pounce, cobras and vipers that strike, pythons that constrict, leeches that suck blood, bees and scorpions that sting and ticks and mosquitos that transmit deadly disease. While all of these risks may be present at Khao Sok National Park, they are greatly exaggerated threats.

Statistically, the most likely cause of serious injury in Thailand's national parks are: 1) motor vehicle accidents and 2) falling from waterfall ledges (usually in a drunken stupor).

Not wanting to dismiss other risks altogether, the following information is provided, not to deter you, but to better ensure your health and safety. Here's a few things to watch out for:

Heat Exhaustion & Stroke:

Don't step off a plane from a cold climate and set off on a rugged rainforest trek without first acclimatizing. Heat exhaustion is brought on by dehydration or salt deficiency from excess sweating. Symptoms include fatigue, lethargy, headaches, giddiness and muscle cramps. Drink sufficient fluids, take salt tablets and always take time to adjust to high temperatures and high humidity.

Heat stroke is a far more serious and, at times, fatal condition when the body's heat regulating system breaks down and body temperatures rise to dangerous levels. Symptoms progress from a general feeling of being unwell to skin becoming flushed and red with little or no sweating. Severe throbbing headaches and lack of coordination may follow. Victims may suffer confusion, become delirious or convulse. Hospitalization is essential. Meanwhile get the victim out of the sun, remove most clothing and reduce temperature by applying a wet sheet or towel, and fan them continously.

Giardia:

This annoying, though not deadly, illness is caused by an intestinal parasite present in water contaminated by animal or human feces. Backpackers have done more to spread this parasite world wide than any other vector. Giardia is still not confirmed for Khao Sok waterways but it may soon be present if it isn't already. Symptoms include stomach cramps, bloated stomach, nausea, frequent gas and watery, foul smelling diarrhea. These symptoms may not appear for several weeks after exposure to the parasite. Metronidazle (marketed as Flagyl) is the recommended drug treatment which should be administered under medical supervision.

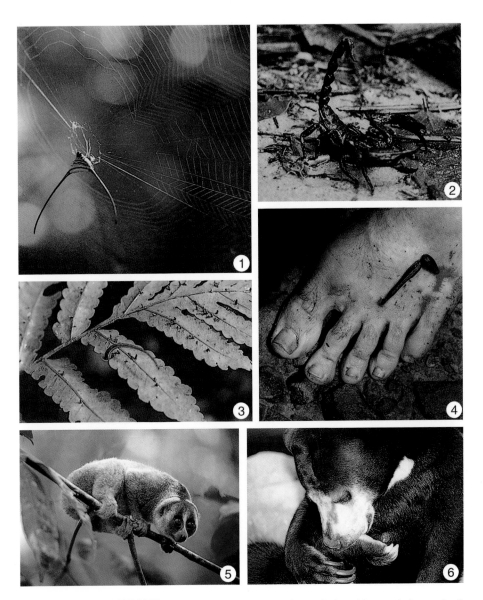

LOOKS CAN BE DECEIVING: *Khao Sok's countless species of web spinning spiders may look menacing 1, but none are poisonous. Scorpions 2 usually have stings no worse than a bee or wasp. While usually regarded as ugly, leeches preying from a leaf 3, or drawing blood 4 are completly harmless in transmitting disease. The cute and cuddly looking Slow Loris 5, on the other hand, has an extremely infectious bite. The Malay Sun bear 6 has huge claws that make it more feared than tigers. Beautiful to behold, the Big-eyed pit viper (page 89) is most active at dusk, and can be deadly.*

The best way to avoid giardia is to only drink purified water. If you are camping always treat river water with purification tablets or bring to a boil. To reduce the risk of giardia spreading at Khao Sok never defecate within 20 meters of a waterway, and be sure it's well buried.

The good news is that there are no parasitic worms or leeches found in the Khao Sok watersheds, or Cheow Lan Lake.

Bee, Wasp & Scorpion Stings:

Unless you are allergic to stings, bees, wasps and scorpions pose little real danger. Most beehives are located high up in huge dipterocarp trees or suspended from overhanging limestone ledges to avoid bear predation. Bee activity is generally restricted to the canopy where flowers are the most abundant. Some wasps and hornets nest in the ground but one is unlikely to disturb them if you stay to established trails.

Scorpions pose little, if any, threat to day hikers as their habits are largely nocturnal. Exercise caution, however, if you are removing leaf litter or wood debris in preparing a campsite. It is also advisable to shake out your boots or shoes before putting them on and check carefully under your bedroll as these shy creatures seek out dark places to hide.

Localized pain, swelling and inflamation are the usual symptoms of these stings. Remove the stinger carefully to avoid additional poison entering the wound. Oral antihistamine tablets can help reduce the pain and swelling and simple pain killers will relieve much of the discomfort. If you are allergic to any type of sting you should consult your doctor for additional precautions.

Leeches & Ticks:

Leeches are common at Khao Sok, especially during the rainy season, but leech bites do not infect (unless excessively scratched) and they transmit no disease. Don't bother wasting time trying to burn them off with a cigarette as they can be peeled off with your fingernail often before they make their tiny incision.

Ticks are far less common at Khao Sok, but should be removed more carefully as they can spread typhus. Gently pull them from the skin.

Cuts & Scratches:

While this may sound too insignificant to mention, these are the most common wounds one is likely to encounter at Khao Sok, and even small wounds can easily become infected in the tropics. Staying to established trails and wearing long trousers, boots and socks are your best defence strategy. If you do get a small wound keep it scrupulously clean and dry and use an antibiotic powder or balm if it shows signs of infection. Serious infections require a visit to a doctor and often a course of antibiotics.

Snake Bite:

Cobras and vipers are among the most venomous snakes found at Khao Sok and, fortunately for the day hiker, they are largely nocturnal. To greatly reduce your chances of ever being bitten wear boots, socks and long trousers, be careful when collecting fire wood and never put your hands into holes, crevices or atop ledges where you cannot see. If you do hike at night use a flashlight.

Though it is rare to even see a poisonous snake at Khao Sok, much less be bitten, if you or a member of your party have this misfortune act promptly but not in a panic. Help the victim to remain calm. Keep assuring them that they will be alright as you gently clean the bite and tie a pressure bandage firmly around the wound. Tensor bandages work well but a ripped sheet or shirt will do. (Tourniquets and sucking out the poison are now discredited procedures.) Once the wound is firmly bound to prevent the spread of the venom it is important to immobilize the limb by splinting above and below the nearest joints, then transport the victim to a hospital. The dead snake is helpful for identifying the correct antivenom for the hospital staff to administer, but don't try to capture the snake if you risk being bitten again. Also keep in mind that snakes do not die easily; people have been struck by seemingly dead (and sometimes beheaded) snakes.

Mosquito Borne Diseases:

Khao Sok is not considered a high risk zone for any of the mosquito borne diseases, and Thailand's control programs in rural areas are among the best in the world. Still it is good to exercise caution as malaria does occur here. The best defence is not a prophylactic but to take precautions to avoid being bitten, especially during peak biting hours just before and after dawn and dusk. Almost all bungalows provide mosquito nets over beds. Insect repellents can offer further day-time protection.

Avoid perfumes and scented aftershares, they do not repel but attract mosquitoes and other biting flies. Wear long-sleeved shirts, long pants, and shoes, especially near dusk. At night sleep under a ceiling fan if possible.

The three mosquito borne diseases found in Southeast Asia, but not necessarily at Khao Sok, are:

1.)   **Malaria** is a virus carried by the mosquito Anopheles. Symptoms may not occur for days, weeks or months after infection. Symptoms usually begin with chills and headache followed by a high fever that lasts sereval hours. Flu symptoms can be very similar so a blood test is required to diagnose malaria.

2.)   **Japanese Encephalitis** is a virus carried by a night-biting mosquito (Culex). There is a greater risk in the rainy season (June - October) especially in rural areas where pigs and birds act as reservoirs for the virus. Symptoms are sudden fever, chills and headache followed by vomiting, delirium, sore joints and muscles and a strong aversion to light. Advanced cases may result in convulsions and coma.

3.)   **Dengue Fever** is a virus transmitted to humans by a day active mosquito (Aedes). Symptoms (which come on suddenly) include: high fever, severe headache, joint and muscle pain. While there is no chemical prophylactic against it, only one in 10,000 mosquitos is infectious. Khao Sok is not a high risk area as there is little standing water for the mosquitos to breed.

Typhus:

Typhus is a disease spread by biting mites and ticks that cling to scrub vegetation in secondary forests. Mountain trekkers can be at risk when walking through heavy brush. Tick and mite repellents like dimethyl phthalate rubbed into the skin every four hours is a good prevention.

All four varieties of typhus cause fever, headache, and skin rash, but intensity of symptoms varies according to type. There is no vaccination, but effective treatment is available if started early enough in the illness.

Animal Bites:

The most common bite one is likely to get at Khao Sok is not a tiger, bear or snake but that of a dog. Most dogs at Khao Sok are stray, avoid them and beware of unusually tame behavior in wild animals. Slow loris, the adorable looking night monkey, will almost certainly bite if touched and their bite is especially infectious. Even the large geckos, when cornered, will bite and you will need medical attention to check for signs of tetanus and dipptheria.

The biggest concern from dog and mammal bites is rabies because after onset the infection is fatal. The time interval between the bite and onset is usually about two months but can vary from a few days to years. Always seek medical advice following an animal bite which breaks the skin.

Hookworm & Hydatid Cysts:

Dogs are not always "man's best friend". Hydatid cysts are contracted by stroking dogs as the larval eggs adhere to a dog's fur. There is no reliable drug treatment for hydatid cysts; they must be surgically removed from the liver where they most often end up being lodged.

Another dog-related problem is "creeping eruption" a syndrome where some hookworm larvae penetrate the skin but can develop no further. They create itchy, red, moving, worm-shaped trails, usually on the feet and legs. Larva currens produces a similar rash on the backside. The worms are contracted by walking barefoot along trails fouled by dogs or sitting in a wet bathing suit beside a waterfall or swimming hole contaminated by dog feces. Think twice about that nice pooch that follows you into the park, and send him home.

SAFE WATERS: No worries mate when it comes to swimming or river crossings at Khao Sok. There are no leeches or dangerous parasites in the water. One little fish with fused teeth does, however, have a penchant for nipping at anything that lingers too long and looks like dead meat. Keep moving.

OTHER PARKS - RIGHT NEXT DOOR

While Khao Sok gets all the hype and fanfare, now designated by the TAT as the number one eco-tourism destination in the south of Thailand, just next door are two adjacent national parks with equal attractions but very few visitors.

Sri Pang Nga National Park borders Khao Sok on its entire western flank. It too has an abundance of wildlife, spectacular waterfalls, and rafflesia flowers, but it receives a fraction of the visitors.

Anyone driving between Takuapa and Khao Sok can't help but admire the continuous forest canopy of Sri Pang Nga National Park, visible to the north of highway 401 as you approach the mountain pass. The only road access to this park, however, is along highway 4, just north of Takuapa on the route to Ranong. Here one can hike along lovely forest paths to view a number of waterfalls: Tam Nang, Ton Ton Sri and Ton Ton Toie.

Some adventure trekking companies at Khao Sok are starting to offer 3 to 4 day off-the-beaten-path adventures that traverse both parks. But even with so few visitors, Sri Phang Nga National Park is being seriously impacted by tourism. Much of the hardwood that has gone into the resort developments of booming Khao Lak has been illegally looted from this park, according to park authorities.

Sri Pang Nga National Park

To Ranong

Khao Pra Mee

Khao Pohta Luang Keaw

Khao Bang Soi

Klong
Nakha Wildlife
Sanctuary

Kuraburi

HWY A

Namtok Tamnang

Namtok Ton Ton Sai

Tamnang Village

Headquarter

Khao Sok National Park

Khao Sok National Park
Headquarter

To Phuket

HWY 401 To Suratthani →

SRI PANG NGA NATIONAL PARK: Primary forests cloak the mountains bordening Khao Sok in a verdant mantle **1**, but visitors here are very few **2**. Tam Nang waterfall **3** is breathtaking in full force (June - Oct), and rafflesia is abundant in bloom (Jan - Mar) **4**.

Klong Phanom National Park borders Khao Sok to the south, just across highway 401. It extends through rugged karst terrain almost as far as Phang - nga Bay. This newly created park attracts even fewer visitors than Sri Pang Nga.

Among the outstanding features of Klong Phanom are stands of massive bamboo, some of which have been used to construct displays at the Visitor Center. Rafflesia flowers are often easier to access in this park than at Khao Sok, and there is believed to be a new species here.

The area is also rich in caves and waterfalls. Dhow Wadung (Waterfall from the Stars), plunges in four spectacular tiers, one of which is a 35 m drop. Visiting this falls requires a 4-day, 3-night trek and a challenging rope descent; it is definitely not one for the tour bus crowds. Wildlife is abundant with many species of hornbills, cats (including tiger), bear, gibbons, langurs, macaques, elephant, deer, tapir and jungle fowl. Some of the caves here also served as communist bunkers during the 70's and 80's.

KEY

① Park Headguarters
② Tham Nam Rot Khao Wang (Communist hide-out cave)
③ Rafflesia flower sites
④ Giant Bamboo
⑤ Elephant Trails
⑥ Dhaw Wadung Waterfall

KLONG PHANOM NATIONAL PARK: *Rugged karst topography 1, massive bamboo 2 and secret "communist" caves 3, are but a few of the outstanding features of Klong Phanom N.P. The third tier of Dhow Wadung (Waterfall from the Stars) plunges in a spectacular 35 m. drop 4.*

PART IV
The Interpretive Trail

HIDDEN WONDERS: *Along the Interpretive Trail one may have the good fortune to view : 1 More than 100 species of nesting song birds, 2 The entrance tunnel of the sweat bee. 3 The lesser mouse deer, one of the world's tinest hoofed animals. 4 Many species of palms including the world's rarest, 5 Amphibians including tree frogs, 6 Wild jungle fowl, the ancestor of the domestic chicken, and 7 The ever elusive and nocturnal serow.*

THE INTERPRETIVE TRAIL

The Khao Sok Interpretive Trail is a public service project of this book in co-operation with Khao Sok National Park. It is designed to acquaint the student and lay person with a number of special features typical of the Southeast Asian rainforest. The 30 trail markers (corresponding with 30 points of text in this book) commence near the Park Headquarters and end approximately 3.5 km into the park at a small island in the Sok River. From here the trail continues on to several popular waterfalls and one is encouraged to further explore on their own, applying the concepts and lessons learned to one's own personal discoveries.

Ideally, an interpretive trail should loop back to the point of origin, but Khao Sok's rugged mountainous terrain is better suited to the hardy explorer than the casual hiker, and the markers have been placed along the route of easiest access. The trail guide, of course, can be followed in either direction; one might choose to study even numbered points of interest on the outbound trip and odd numbered markers on the return trip.

NOTE: Because rainforest eco-systems are in a dynamic state of flux the numbered markers that correspond with this text may not always be sequential. A termite mound may be destroyed by a bear for instance, or a wild banana may start growing where a towering emergent tree recently crashed to the ground. Expect surprises in the forest and in the number sequence as well.

There are several side trails worth exploring along this route with special features noted. Feel free to explore these routes, but please stay to the trails. These first few kilometers into the park receive the heaviest use and restricting oneself to established trails greatly minimizes the impact. It also better guarantees your safety.

Please note and observe the Khao Sok Hiking Trail Etiquette Guidelines listed on pages 68 & 69 and do your part to keep this experience a rewarding one for all nature lovers and all of nature.

Khao Sok
Interpretive Trail
Guide

1. KARST FORMATIONS

The dramatic "karst" formations, visible through the foilage here, distinguish Khao Sok National Park more than any other topographic feature. These massive limestone uplifts were once part of an ancient coral reef system that stretched from China down through Vietnam, Laos, Thailand, and into northern Borneo.

Thriving as living coral communities 225-280 millions years ago, they made up a reef system five times longer than Australia's Great Barrier Reef. Uplifting of the Earths crust combined with constant erosion from fluctuating sea levels and monsoon rains has resulted in the spectacular shapes you see before you.

Karst topography is generally honey-combed with extensive cave systems providing habitat for the millions of bats which play such a key role in Southeast Asian rainforest ecology.

Humans, too, have directly benefited from karst cave systems. The oldest human habitation sites in Southeast Asia are found here dating back 50,000 years.

Some of these caves display beautiful pre-historic cave paintings and ancient burial sites.

The plant communities which colonize karst formations are specially adapted to limestone, lack of (or impoverished) soils, and long periods of dryness. Decomposing leaves from these plants combine with heavy seasonal rainfall to produce a slightly acid water which readily dissolves the limestone. The beautiful stalactites and stalagmites visible both within the caves and on the outer faces of the karsts are a result of this steady acid water erosion carrying away and depositing calcium carbonate.

Karst formations in Thailand are most pronounced in Krabi, Phangnga and here in Surat Thani provinces. Khao Sok National Park boasts some of the world's most spectacular formations of this kind along the shores of the vast Cheow Lan Lake (reservoir) which forms the parks northeastern boundary.

Bird nest fern

2. EPIPHYTES

Primary tropical rainforests typically do not support a shrub level as is common in temperate forests. The sparse understory here is almost exclusively made up of saplings stuggling through the darkness to find a place in the sun. One group of plants has evolved a strategy to bypass this competitive struggle to reach the light; they simply spend their entire life cycle in the forest canopy. They are called epiphytes.

Look up at the rich array of plant life growing along the branches and crutches of trees. These plants are not parasitic, but epiphytic, i.e. they merely use the trees as a perch to take advantage of full light. When epiphytes fall to the ground as a result of being torn off their perch in high winds, torrential rain, animal distrubance or other causes, they usu-

ally perish in the darkness of the forest floor.

The largest and most dramatic of the epiphytes are ferns : Bird nest fern (Aspienuim ridus), Staghorn fern (Platycerium holttumii) and Kite fern (Drynaria guercifolia). These attractive plants reproduce by spores which are carried on the wind and take root in the bark of a tree. As they grow many species of epiphytic ferns create a basket of living and dead leaves which act to trap nutrients from leaves and debris falling from trees overhead. Such ferns are also able to absorb and store huge quantities of water, so much so that at times of heavy rain the weight of epiphytic ferns can become more than the tree can bear and the limbs, or the entire tree, are brought crashing to the ground.

The Bird nest fern derives its name from the fact that some bird species, namely pittas and the larger owls, often use these platforms as nest sites. The Staghorn fern gets its name from the multiple branching fronds that resemble stag antlers. Kite fern, or *Hua Wow*, derives its Thai name from the fact that children use the dry fern fronds to make small kites to fly at rice harvest time.

Both the Bird nest and Staghorn ferns are highly prized as ornamentals in Thai gardens and consequently have been largely looted from National Park boundaries. The specimens you see overhead are part of a reintroduction effort. These plants were salvaged and relocated here from an old oil palm plantation that was being cut down in a neighbouring province.

Orchids are perhaps the most famous of all epiphytes but are rarely seen in the rainforest because of their height in the

Staghorn fern

canopy. In montane forests where they achieve the same level of light, rainfall and high humidity as at lower levels, they are closer to the ground and are more commonly observed. Unlike ferns, orchids fix their nitrogen directly from the air and do not depend on trapping leaf litter for nutrients.

3. PANDANUS

This is an outsanding example of Pandanus, a member of the family Pandanaceae which ranges from the coast to deep interior tropical forests. The fruit of this plant is large, (shaped somewhat like a pineapple) and comprised of numerous phalanges which are reddish-yellow when ripe. It is an important food source for civets, squirrel, porcupine, deer and wild pig. The strong leaf blades are stripped of their saw-toothed edges and woven into durable floor mats used in households throughout Thailand and Southeast Asia.

4. WILD GINGER

One of the most delighfful flavors in Thai cuisine comes from the root stock of these attractive forest plants. Wild ginger (Zingiber) has a large rhizome, i.e. a horizontal underground stem, that is swollen with food reserves. The rhizome contains oils and resins which give the pungent properties so essential in flavouring food. Ginger prefers moist, well drained soils and partial sunlight. There are different species growing along this trail system and while flowers vary greatly, the leaf patterns are similar.

Thai ginger, (Zingiber spectabile), seen growing here, is commonly used in cooking as is torch ginger (Phaeomevia magnifica) and red ginger (Alpinia purpurata). All three species display lovely red and pink flowers.

Golden orb spider

5. GIANT SPIDERS, WEAVER ANTS &
SWEAT BEES

Some of the most common and interesting features along this trail are habitats created by spiders, ants, termites and bees. The life cycle of insects is much too short, of course, for this marker to have any real relevance (short of chance) to these habitats being in the immediate vicinty. Take the time here to learn about them, nontheless, as you will surely encounter the handiwork of one or more of these insects during your walk.

The golden orb spider is so large and constructs such massive and strong webs that some speculate they feed on small birds as well as insects. For this reason it is also known as the "bird-eating spider." The female of this species is exceptionally large and beautifully colored while the male is only a fraction of her size. Look for the giant webs overhead and alongside the trail; they are most common.

The tunnel spider is also very common, and easy to view along the cut-away embankments beside the road way. Look for concentrated webbing narrowing down into a tunnel shaft where the spider darts in hasty retreat at the first sign of your movement.

Weaver ants are but one of thousands of ant species found in the rainforest, but their habitats are unique. This widely-foraging large red ant constructs its nest from living leaves on trees and shrubs. Weaver ants can lock their jaws and legs together in such a way as to bridge open space. This ability allows them to pull together a series of leaves to contruct their nest chamber. The leaves are literally sewn together  with a silk-like thread that the adult ants squeeze from the larvae of their young.

Weaver ants normally do not bite unless one threatens their nest site at which time they become merciless. If you accidentally come into contact with one of their nest trees, you will soon know it. Brush off the biting ants, step back, and trace the column of angry ants back to the well-camouflaged nest. Weaver ant eggs are considered a real delicacy and are much sought after in some parts of Thailand.

Trigonid or sweat bees are another interesting insect you may see swarming about your body as you hike through this forest. Don't worry, these little bees dont sting, they're merely attracted to the salts in your sweat. Try to follow the path of these bees back to their hive and you will discover a remarkable entrance chamber built from wax and the resin of the tree the bee inhabits.

Forest dwellers, like the Mani tribes people, use sweat bee tunnels as a fire starter. The sweat bee, however, has fared far better than these nomadic, hunter-gatherer peoples who may have once inhabited this region. The last nomadic bands of Mani remaining in Thailand are now restricted to a few fringes of forest in Trang and Satun provinces.

Great hornbill

6. WILD FRUIT AND HORNBILLS

Many trees native to the Southeast Asian tropical forest produce highly prized fruits such as the wild jackfruit tree (Antocarpus heterophylla) standing here. Mangosteen (Garcinia mangostana), Durian (Durio zibethinus), Rambutan (Nepheliuim lappaceum), Jujube (Zizyphus jujuba) and Pomelo (Citrus grandis), are among other world-renowned delicacies native to these rainforests.

There are literally hundreds of other edible and choice rainforest fruits that have been eaten by forest dwelling tribes for 50,000 years but still remain unknown to the rest of the world. Penan children, on the island of Borneo, can list the names of 100-200 wild forest fruits they consume on a regular basis. Most educated people would be hard pressed to come up with a list of 30 fruits they know of worldwide.

Forest dwellers such as the Mentawai people of Siberut Island, Indonesia, do not leave jackfruit propagation to mere chance, but selectively breed and plant seeds of only the sweetest tasting fruits. Their gardens are literally the forest itself. Much more important than humans as propagators of rainforest fruits is the hornbill. The hornbill is the name of a family (Bucerotide) of large, Old World, tropical birds which have enormous curved bills and often a bony cask on the head. Thirty of the world's 54 species of hornbill occur in Asia with thirteen species found in Thailand. Khao Sok has five confirmed species of hornbill including the rare helmeted hornbill (Rhinoplax vigil).

The hornbill is a true keystone species. As fruit eaters they are critical to seed dispersal; without them the forest would not be as luxuriant or diverse.

Cut away view of nest chamber

The presence of hornbills in large numbers is a good indicator of the health of the forest, and a healthy forest in turn allows hornbills to thrive. As a survivor the hornbill is in a class of its own. Living relics from at least fifteen million years ago, the hornbill as a species is one of the oldest birds surviving on Earth.

Some people, and Thai advertising agencies, frequently confuse hornbills with toucans – a New World species found in Central and South American tropical forests. Both bird species have enormous bills and both nest in tree cavities, but they belong to totally unrelated familes. The toucan is related to woodpeckers, hornbills to kingfishers.

It is common to hear the calls of various hornbills and the "whosk, whosk whosk" sound of the wings as they fly above the canopy at Khao Sok. Look for hornbills frequenting trees in fruit especially in the morning and evening as many birds use the same daily flight paths. Perhaps the greatest sighting of all is the great hornbill, (Buceros bicornis). It has a look so majestic it has caused naturalists to remark that if ever there was royalty in the bird kingdom, the great hornbill would be king. Massive in size, the casque of this bird branches into two, giving the species its name of (two horns). The bill, face, and chest of the great hornbill are painted a bright yellow from a gland at the base of the tail, which the bird can reach with its long bill. Adorned with dramatic yellow paint and black and white plummage, the overall appearance of the great hornbill is quite regal.

Great hornbills mate for life and, like all hornbills, nest in hollow tree cavities. The hornbill cannot excavate these holes despite their impressive bill, but must rely on natural cavities where a limb tore out, or a bear excavated a beehive, usually in large dipterocarp trees.

When the breeding season arrives in January, the male will search out such a tree hole and take the female for approval. If accepted the female will enter the chamber and proceed to be locked in by plastering the entrance with a mixture of mud, tree bark, wooddust, food debris and even her own feces. A narrow vertical opening in the plaster, just big enough to be fed and defecate through, but too small for snakes, monitor lizards, civets or other predators to enter, is the desired result. From the time the nest is sealed until the chicks become fledglings (approx 60-90 days) the female and the brood are fully dependent on the male for all their food.

The male hornbill is an amazing provider. A great hornbill was once observed filling his crop with more than 200 figs at a time which were later regurgitated for the female and chicks back at the nest site. As the chicks grow they require more protein: insects, frogs, lizards, snakes and even other species of birds become food. The female does not accept everything the male brings her, but selectively chooses what is best for her chicks. After months of voluntary confinement, the female finally pecks her way out of the increasingly cramped nest hole and both parents begin the task of teaching their young to forage for themselves. For millions of years hornbills have been a model for good parenting.

(See photos of unique cliff nesting behavior at Khao Sok, page 18)

Pitta nest in Salacca palm

7. RATTAN PALM

Southeast Asia's tropical forests support more than 100 plant familes with several thousand tree species, the greatest botanical diversity on Earth. If there is one family, however, that is the unchallenged winner of the diversity contest, that family is Palmee – the palms.

More than 1,300 species of palm grow in this realm, again the greatest concentration in the world. Some palms are medium-sized trees like the coconut, bettlenut and choke palm. Others are small trees of the understory like the clock palms so common in the Khao

Sok forest. Still others are lianas, like the climbing rattan palm you see here.

This particular species of rattan has evolved a very effective strategy for working its way quickly up into the light rich realm of the canopy. Note the long, slender (almost invisible) tendrils covered in miniature barbs which this rattan palm dangles. The liana is in some sense fishing with these hooks, hoping to catch hold of a faster growing plant that can help pull it up and lend support on its climb toward the light. The barbed tendrils work equally well in preventing the vine from falling during typhoon winds and when failing limbs strike against the rattan. Instead of crashing all the way down to the forest floor, the barbs usually stop the fall at an advantageous upper level of the canopy.

Rattan vines are amazingly strong yet flexible, both excellent qualities for crafting them into beautiful rattan furniture. Rattan harvesters scrape away the thorny outer bark exposing a smooth green bark which turns a polished brown not long after it is cut. By steaming the rattan it can be bent into fantastic shapes even after it has dried. Rattan harvesting has long been an important renewable forest industry for both forest-dwelling tribes and lowland farmers living near forest areas. Attempts to raise rattan in plantation settings have yet to prove successful.

Some endangered species are very dependent on thorny palms. Gurney's pitta, for instance, builds its nests in thick clusters of Salacca palm where the razor sharp thorns protect the eggs and offsprings from foraging snakes, civets, jungle cats and other predators. The Gurney's pitta was believed extinct for thirty years but has now been found living at two locations in Krabi province, and may possibly be resident at Khao Sok.

8. CANOPY LEVELS

From this vantage point you can look back down the Sok River bordered by a verdant expanse of tropical forest. Although natural ecosystems–tropical ones in particular, are so immensely complex they defy simple description, there is a tendency for humans to want to put some semblence of order to things. Describing the sophisticated tapestry of a tropical rainforest in various levels is one such attempt.

Biologists generally recognize five levels of a rainforest : 1) emergent trees which rise above the canopy 2) the upper canopy 3) the lower canopy 4) the under story and 5) the forest floor. For our purposes we will consider two more niches: the aerial space above the forest canopy, and the subterranean level below the forest floor.

A. ABOVE THE CANOPY

Look up and you will likely see swiftlets soaring through the air in search of high-flying insects. Swiftlets occupy this niche by day while insectiverous bats patrol these skies by night. These animals share their habitats in nearby caves, exchanging residence every dawn and dusk.
Eagles, hawks and falcons also hunt from this high vantage point. There is no real habitat here, but it is an important niche in the forest ecosystem.

A

B

C

D

E

F

G

B. EMERGENT TREES

Looking out over the expanse of rainforest before you, note how some trees stand high above the rest. These are the emergents, usually of the dipterocarp family. These massive trees may rise forty meters or more from the forest floor and may be several centuries old. They are the preferred trees for gibbons when singing, grooming and sleeping, and they provide excellent habitat for hornbill nesting cavities.

C. UPPER CANOPY

Most of what you see in the distance is the upper canopy of the forest, the preferred habitat of sunbirds, flowerpeckers, barbets, fruit doves and hornbills. Bees and leaf feeding insects are prolific in this realm where 50% of all species on Earth (most of them insects) are found.
Mammals which prefer the upper canopy are: fruit bats, large squirrels, gibbons, langurs, and flying lemur.

D. LOWER CANOPY

Just below the upper canopy is a layer of forest formed by the crowns of shorter trees. Here butterflies are found in abundance as are tree frogs and gliding lizards. Woodpeckers, trogons, flycatchers and bulbuis are the main bird species found here. Mammals which prefer the lower canopy are: clouded leopard, slow loris, civets, tree shrews and smaller squirrels.

E. UNDERSTORY

Low-growing ferns, palms, bamboo, herbs and young saplings make up the sparse understory of primary tropical rainforest. Relatively easy to traverse and rich in succulent forage, this is the preferred habitat of large grazers and their predators: elephants, rhino, sambar deer, barking deer, mouse deer, bear, tiger, porcupine, and marten.

F. FOREST FLOOR

The forest floor is a realm largely reserved for insects and decomposers: beetles, scorpions, ants, millipedes, leeches, and insectiverous mammals such as the scaley anteater.

G.SUBTERRANEAN

Below the forest floor lie burrowing animals such as bamboo rats, snakes such as cobras, and burrowing spiders like tarantulas. Cicada nymphs spend most of their life cycle here as do the grubs of other beetles and many species of termites.

9. SECONDARY FOREST

The scrub-like forest you see here is secondary forest – a "jungle" in the truest sense of the word. Note the almost impenetrable tangle of vegetation that prohibits passage for all but the most intrepid, machete-wielding, hero of Hollywood adventure films.

By contrast, the primary forest you will enter at the end of this roadway is relatively open and easy to pass through as most of the dense vegetation is high overhead in the canopy. Rainforest and jungle are quite different habitats, though the terminology is frequently used interchangeably by the uninformed.

This patch of secondary forest resulted from early attempts to log this region before Khao Sok National Park was established in 1980. In 1989 Thailand proclaimed a nation-wide ban on commerical logging following devastating floods and landslides from denuded slopes in southern Thailand that killed more than 100 people.

This forest clearing, fortunately, is not that large and is similar in size to openings created by natural circumstances such as violent storms. Even the natural death and fall of a huge emergent tree in the forest can create an opening of comparable size.

Some plant species have evolved strategies to quickly colonize these clearings with such properties as: wind-borne seeds, light-tolerant saplings and rapid growth. It will take more than a century to fully restore this site to a 'primary" condtion, dominated by towering dipterocarps and other species, but the process of successive forest stages is already advanced.

Note the lovely melastoma shrubs with their pink blossoms attracting butterflies and nectar-sipping sun birds. Some forest species adapt very well to small forest clearings. Many smaller birds you may see here actually thrive in secondary forest communities. Others, like the hornbills, only come back if old trees with breeding cavities remain, and there is ample fruit in the surrounding old growth forest to sustain them.

Golden babbler

10. RAFFLESIA & PALM LANGKOW

The trail up Bang Luk Chang (Baby Elephant Creek) leads off from the roadway here and at one time ended 1.5 km up a steep ridge at the site of the rafflesia flower (Rafflesia Kerri Meijer).

This is truly an endemic species trail as it features another unique plant – Palm langkow.

Once you have passed the lowland section of the trail where several massive trees grow along the creek embankment you will start to see Palm langkow growing on the hillside which the trail ascends. Notice how some of the fan-shaped leaves have been perforated in a circle near the stem and collapsed like a folded umbrella. This is the handiwork of

Palm langkow blade
modified by bat

Palm langkow (Kerriodoxa elegans) is a small (3-5 m) tall, attractive palm with large fan-shaped leaves with silver-white undersides which eminate from a central thick trunk. It is found at Khao Sok and Khao Phra Taew forest park, Phuket, and nowhere else on Earth. The International Union for the Conservation of Nature (IUCN) lists it as the world's most endangered palm species.

a bat which is constructing its own shelter. The bat has yet to be identified but could very well be new to science.

A few short years ago one could continue on up the trail to see a raffiesia flower site. The buds were visible on the host liana from October to December and the flowers were in bloom for a few short days January to February. Today the site may never recover from so much abuse.

Rafflesia, or *buahpoot* as it is locally called, is Thailand's largest flower and one of the world's rarest and most unusual plants. It was first collected in 1927 and 1929 from four locations in South Thailand. Recent studies have confirmed the species distribution in Khao Sok National Park and the adjacent Klong Nakka Wildlife Sancturary. Current evidence suggests that this species is confined to southern Tenasserim Hills in Thailand's provinces of Chumphon, Ranong and Surat Thani.

Rafflesia is a parasitic plant with no roots or leaves of its own. It invades lianas of the genus Tetvastigma (Vitaceae) and, like a fungus, it absorbs all of its nutrients from its host. Once a year small flower buds begin to develop beneath the root bark of the woody liana. As they mature the buds break through the root and swell to the size of a soccer ball. The flower blooms in a spectacular display of color (ochre, yellow, chestnut and white), and enormous size (up to 80 cm in diameter).

The flower emits a sickly sweet smell, a bit like a rotting carcass, which attracts flies for pollination. A female flower must be pollinated by a male flower, no simple task considering how rare and widely spaced the blooms may be. To further compound reproduction problems, rafflesia only blooms for 3-4 days, then turns black and shrivels away like a rotting mushroom.

No one is yet totally certain how seeds are dispersed to infect a new host liana, but botanists do know that the plant is restricted to the Sundaic region of Southeast Asia, and that it is endangered and easily damaged or destroyed.

It is well documented that sites where rafflesia have been taken by local villagers for curios, food or medicinal use do not regenerate new flowers in subsequent years. Whether a site trampled by eco tourists can recover remains to be seen.

11. DRIP TIPS & EPIPHYLLAE

Look at the wealth of vegetation all around you. It is extremely difficult, even for trained botanists, to bring order to this scene, much less identify all the species present here. There are, nonetheless, some general guidelines.

waxy-surfaced, and with elongated tips. These "drip tips" offer a means by which leaves can rapidly shed water and direct the moisture down toward the plants root system. Rainfall, dew and fog are so prevalent in these forests that were it not for the rapid shedding of water from the leaf, other plants would start to colonize its surface. That is exactly what is happening with some of the plants nearby.

Note the tiny, almost microscopic, mosses, algae and lichens which colonize these leaf surfaces. They are not parasitic, but merely taking adavntage of the abundant leaf moisture and their host plant's hard-earned place in the sun. While the host plant is not deprived of nutrients, it does have some of its leaf surface blocked from the sunlight it requiries. These colonies of tiny epiphytic plants are known as epiphyllae.

It is the rule, rather than the exception, that every tree species in the tropical forest is surrounded by unrelated species. It is also true that the greater the rainfall in a tropical forest the greater the diversity of plants. A third ground rule is that plants belonging to completely different families will share common features.

Leaves, for instance, share many similar characteristics. They tend to be large,

As you work your way along the trail take note of the seemingly infinite variations of leaf shapes and their specialized "drip tips". Sketch a few of your favorites in the space beside these drawings. Better yet, design a leaf shape completely from your imagination and see if it doesn't have a similar counterpart here in this forest.

12. STRANGLER FIG

One of the most peculiar plants of the tropical rainforest is the strangler fig which is not a tree at all but rather a liana vine. Like most fig species, the strangler fig produces copious amounts of fruit which is gorged on by many species of birds, monkeys, gibbons, squirrels, slow loris, bats and other canopy feeding animals.

Because fig fruit is a potent laxative, the tiny seeds pass through the digestive tracks of these animals quite quickly and the sticky feces is spread throughout the forest canopy. A fig seed that lands on a tree branch with ample light and moisture has the right conditions to germinate and send roots down the trunk of the tree. Once the roots reach the ground and are able to take advantage of added

branches thereby stealing their host's sunlight. A liana vine has now become one of the emergents in the forest.

It may take a century or more for a strangler fig to completely enclose and kill its host tree. The host dies from lack of light more than strangulation, and once it rots away the fig "tree" is left standing with a hollow center. If you should come across a fallen strangler fig trunk you can walk or crawl through it like a tunnel.

Fortunately, for the myriad animals that depend on its fruit, strangler figs have no commercial timber value whatsoever, and are usually left standing following selective logging operations.

nutrients, the fig grows quickly, the roots increase in number and they begin to fuse together on contact with one another. Eventually they completely encircle the host tree's trunk and spread a huge umbrella-shaped crown above its

One of the best ways to observe birds and small mammals, both diurnal and nocturnal species, is to find a fruiting fig tree, erect a concealed watch place at a good vantage point, then sit back and await the animals.

Squirrels, bats and birds sip banana flower nectar

13. WILD BANANA

Wild banana appear naturally in forest clearings where large trees have toppled, or along riverbanks with full sunlight. Like the coconut (Cocos nucifera) the wild banana originated in the Southeast Asian forests and has been spread pan-tropically by man.

Note the very small size of the fruit, but the exceptionally large seed as compared to our domesticated hybrids. The wild banana is fed on by many forest creatures: palm civets, monkeys, elephant, squirrel, jungle cats, flying fox (fruit bats) and many fruit eating birds. Look for signs of animals feeding here such as partially eaten fruit and animal droppings. Look also at the undersides of the large banana leaves. Small bats frequently roost on the underside of these natural umbrellas.

Wild bananas are good colonizing plants

and readily fill any new forest clearing by way of sucker shoots they put up from underground. To colonize a new site, however, the banana is wholly dependent on seed dispersal by animals, hence their attractive and delicious fruit.

In addition to sweet fruit, the banana also produces a flower which feeds nectar sipping birds, squirrels and bats and is a favourite in many Thai dishes. Banana leaves are widely used as food wrappings and place settings by both forest dwelling tribes and rural Thai people. Even the banana stalk has a revered place in Thai culture. For seven centuries, cross-sections of banana stalk with their hollow air chambers have been used to make floats (krathongs) for Loi Krathong, a beautiful ceremony which pays homage to the goddess of water on the full moon of the 12th lunar month.

14. BAMBOO GROVES & ELEPHANTS

Bamboo groves are one of the most common features along this trail system. Bamboo is a grass of the family Graminece, like rice and sugarcane, there are more than 1,500 species in this family. Bamboo is the oldest grass on Earth, dating back 60 million years. It is also the largest grass (up to 10 meters) and one of the fastest growing plants on Earth. Some species can grow more than a meter in a 24 hour period. Bamboo spreads by underground root stocks or rhizomes, so it usually appears

in large clumps. Rhizomes of bamboo hold soil very tenaciously, preventing soil erosion on hillsides and riverbanks. The massive foilage absorbs the impact of torrential rains and the leaf litter makes excellent mulch, preventing moisture loss while increasing the soil's organic content. Depending on the species, once every 17 to 40 years, bamboo will go to seed and then die back. (There was a massive die back of bamboo along this trail system in late 1995). The seeds are spread by wind allowing bamboo to colonize large areas much faster than by producing rhizomes.

While bamboo is commonplace in monsoon forest (i.e. forests with distinct dry and wet seasons) it is not found extensively in primary rainforest- unless the site has been disturbed as was the case along this road way. Another explanation for the predomi- nance of bamboo in this area is the fact that Khao Sok National Park lies in the transition zone between the monsoon forests of northern Thailand (which have an annual dry spell of 2-6 months), and the prevalent if langurs have recently frequented this site.

Eight species of leaf monkeys or langurs are found in the Sundaic subregion of Southeast Asia. The most common species seen at Khao Sok are the silver leaf monkey and the dusky leaf monkey, a lowland forest species here at the northern limit of its range. The dusky langur has big black eyes in large white eye patches and, like all langurs, a tail longer than its body.

Khao Sok's wild elephants also feed heavily on bamboo in this area. As one might expect the world's largest land

Dusky langur

true tropical "rainforest" of South Thailand, Malaysia, Sumatra and Borneo in which rain falls in every month of the year.

Bamboo foilage is a favourite food of leaf monkeys or langurs which often sleep in the branches of bamboo overhanging this trail. Look for fresh droppings on the road way and note the strong "zoo-like" odor which is very

mammal is no light eater, consuming up to 250 kg each day. The local herd of five adult cows, one old matriarch and two calves frequent this part of the trail during the rainy season (June-Oct). Note where sections of bamboo look like a bulldozer has run through it. From November to May this herd is usually seen near the reservoir, presumably to avoid the heavier traffic of visitors during peak season on this trail.

There are 33,000 wild elephants in Southeast Asia with an estimated 100 which still roam the wilds of Khao Sok and its adjacent wildlife sanctuaries. Should you have the great good fortune of seeing these magnificent beasts in the wild exercise extreme caution. A 4-6 ton animal that can charge through with each other within a distance of 3 km. The sound elephants produce is usually beyond the range of human hearing. Most wandering and foraging is done at night. Asian elephants are slightly smaller than their African counterparts but are superbly adapted to forest environments.

They feed on bamboo, coconut shoots, sugarcane, palm trunks, riverside grasses, leaves, bark, roots and fruit. They are good swimmers and are able to cross bodies of water several kilometers wide. Fishermen on Cheow Lan Lake tell of elephant herds swimming in the moonlight to access some of the offshore islands covered in bamboo. In addition to its benefits to wildlife, bamboo provides great benefits to man. Strong, fast growing, easily harvested and amazingly adaptable, bamboo is the forest at 40 km/hour is not one to take lightly. The females are very protective of their young, and the lone bulls can be easily annoyed. Don't approach or pursue them, but quietly back off until they pass by. Elephants have a lifespan nearly the same as humans and can communicate used to make everything from rafts to bungalows, fish traps to fences, scaffolding to plumbing, and furniture to cooking pots and eating utensils. And yes you can even eat it; bamboo shoot salad is a local delicacy.

Javan rhino

15. RHINOCEROUS CREEK

This small tributary of the Sok River marks the end of the road way and the beginning of the more interesting and intimate trail system. From here the interpretive trail continues on for another kilometer to a small island in the Sok River.

A short hike downstream from the confluence of this creek and the Sok River is a small waterfall (Wing Hin) best viewed during the rainy season (June-October). You must ford the Sok River to access the falls.

It is interesting that theThai name for this creek "Bang Hua Raed" means Rhinocerous Creek, though this mammal is not listed as one of Khao

Sok's 48 confirmed mammal species. Local farmers and guides speak confidently of the rhino's former presence in this region as late as the early 1980's although none have been sighted in recent years.

The Sumatran and Java rhino are endangered throughout their range not only because of servere habitat loss with the felling of the once vast rainforests, but largely because of the illegal trade in rhino horn. Highly prized in Chinese apothecary shops, powdered rhino horn is today worth more than its weight in gold.

Sumatran and Javan rhino were once so abundant in Thailand's tropical forests that in the 1800s Thailand was exporting nearly 1,000 per year to China. By 1977 the Java rhino was considered extinct in Thailand and the Sumatran rhino seriously endangered. The Sumatran rhino, unlike the Asian elephant, lives exclusively in the tropical rainforest. This huge herbivore is a largely solitary creature with each individual requiring approximately 10 square km of forest to meet their huge dietary needs of ginger stem, palm heart, broad-leafed herbs and twigs of various trees. Whether the Sumatran rhino still exists in some remote parts of Khao Sok National Park is open to debate. The sad truth is that poaching of many endangered species is widespread throughout Thailand with parks and wildlife sanctuaries as the prime targets.

At Khao Yai National Park, Thailand's first and one of its largest protected areas, there is known to be a direct and inverse relation between the distance from park headquarters and the protection accorded the park's wildlife. There are far more gibbons, deer and tiger, for instance, near the heavily visited tourist areas of the park than there are in the remote reaches where poachers can operate with little fear of detection.

Unfortunately, the same may be true of Khao Sok. Tourism in these areas, while certainly not without impact, may be the strongest deterrent to illegal wildlife hunting. Currently under intense poaching threats here at Khao Sok are: elephant for ivory, tiger for teeth and bones, clouded leopard for fur coats, hornbill for the ivory in their casque and meat, gibbons for pets, deer for meat and antler, and bear for medicinal gall bladders, claws and meat. Asiatic black bear and Malay sun bear are especially prized by Koreans who gather around large banquet tables in Bangkok while the bears are literally cooked alive before them.

Animal rights groups and conservationists in Thailand are working hard to stop this slaughter. Please report to Park Headquarters anyone you may see, or even suspect, is poaching plants or wildlife from this area. A word of caution, however; don't intervene directly. More than one park ranger in Thailand has been killed in the line of duty.

Clouded leopard

16. WILD PEPPER

The attractive, tear-drop shaped leaves of the small vine growing here is wild pepper. Try not to disturb this woody climber too much in looking for tendrils of flowers and fruit. If you find green and red peppercorn seeds growing please don't pick them, but leave the seed to reproduce and for others to view.

Black pepper, ginger, cinnamon and cloves were among the fabled spices of Southeast Asian rainforests which drew Arab, and later Europeans to this part of the world. It is interesting to think that the entire Western Hemisphere was an accidental discovery by European explorers just trying to gain direct access to these humble plants.

Today most pepper is grown commercially in plantations on 2-3 meter posts where the plant takes on a bushy columnar appearance. In the wild, the pepper vine will grow to heights in excess of 10 meters. The fruit is dull green when young, turning red when ripe and black when fully dried. Black and green pepper corn are used extensively in Thai cooking and for centuries were one of the hottest components. The fiery red chilli pepper is a European introduction to Asia from Central America following colonization of the New World. Once the Thais had access to this new spice, they quickly became successful at breeding one of the hottest chilli peppers in the world.

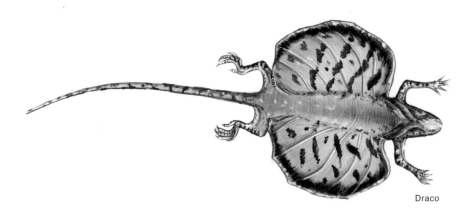

Draco

17. GLIDING LIZARDS, LEMURS & SQUIRRELS

As impenetrable as the rainforest canopy may appear looking up from below, there are sizeable gaps between tree crowns. Some smaller mammals, reptiles and amphibians have thus evolved abilities to glide as an economical and rapid way of getting about in the treetops. There are gliding squirrels, lemurs, lizards, frogs and even snakes – all able to cross great distances of open space. By evolving an ability to glide, all of these species not only conserve energy but avoid unnecessary, and potentially dangerous, trips to the ground when feeding or fleeing from tree to tree.

Gliding squirrels and lemurs are largely nocturnal by nature because their aerial acrobatics in daylight would present predators with too easy a target. Flying lemurs, of course, don't really fly at all, but can glide up to 130 meters through the forest in a shallow dive. They do this by climbing a tree in a rather awkward fashion, encumbered as they are by the folds in their gliding membrane. On reaching a suitable tree height they glide

gradually down to a lower level on another tree. They then must begin the labourous climb up all over again. This gliding feat is especially impressive for female flying lemurs as they carry their single young, firmly attatched to their bellies when in flight.

Flying lemurs are not really lemurs at all but form an order dermoptere (meaning skin wings) uniquely their own. There are only two species in this unusual order, both are restricted to Southeast Asia, and one (Cynocephalus variegatus) is found here at Khao Sok. You can look for these amazing mammals near dusk and gliding from tree to tree throughout the night, but they are not easy to spot. The giant flying squirrel (Petaurista alborefus) is another aerial wonder. A membrane of skin stretched between all four limbs acts as a parachute enabling them to glide remarkable distances. Flying squirrels do all of their foraging for fruit and nectar at night and can be observed with a torch or halogen lamp, and a good deal of luck.

The flying lizard (Draco sp) also uses a

Flying squirrel

skin membrane to glide, but unlike the flying lemur and flying squirrel, the skin is stretched across ribs which extend dramatically from the belly. Flying lizards are active throughout the daylight hours which allows them to be frequently observed along this trail. Unless one has a very keen eye, however, it is almost impossible to detect these superbly camouflaged reptiles against a tree trunk.

Only when viewed in profile, while scurrying around a tree, or actually in flight, do they tend to catch the eye. Even when gliding Draco may resemble nothing more than a falling leaf, and indeed they seem to time their movements from tree to tree when winds send dead leaves fluttering from the canopy to the ground. Now that you know what to look for, see if you can spot one or more. They're common here.

The Malaysian flying tree snake (Chrysopelea) achieves its unlikely aerial abilities by flattening its body and making lateral writhing movements as it launches up to 50 meters through open space. There are even flying frogs in the rainforest – some with membranes between the limbs, other species with very large webbed feet upon which they can soar 12 meters or more.

It is interesting to speculate how birds, with the full ability to fly may have evolved from reptiles that glide. Though there are many mammals that glide, there is only one mammal that can truly fly – the bat, and they make up nearby 20% of all mammal species.

18. CICADA LIFE CYCLE

One rainforest animal that you have undoubtedly heard, if not seen, is the cicada. That high-pitched, buzz-saw sound which comes and goes, or completely surrounds you, is the love song of the male cicada earnestly trying to attract a mate. For all of its intensity, this is only a brief, impassioned moment in the sun during this insect's largely subterranean life cycle.

A cicada nymph may spend up to 15 years below the forest floor, slowly developing and molting into a wingless form which then crawls its way to the surface through a tunnel. (Look for these cicada mud castings throughout the forest as they are common in certain areas.)

Upon reaching the surface, the nymph then works its way up the trunk of a nearby tree or sapling, locks its feet firmly to the bark and undergoes yet another metamorphosis. The back splits open longtitudinally and the adult cicada emerges with a double pair of translucent wings. Both male and female are now free to fly and seek out mates.

Cicadas sing by contracting their thorax up to 1,000 times per second. Only male cicadas sing and they do so for the singular purpose of attracting females. .Fortunately for the females, (and us) not all species sing at the same time. Females would never find the right males (and humans might likely go deaf) if all of those ear-splitting frequencies were overlapping one another at once. So cicadas have developed a very practical solution to their din: the males adhere to strict times of day for each species to broadcast its sound.

The day begins at Khao Sok with the song of a cicada that has been compared to a smoke detector going off. The last cicada of the day sings in flight just as it's growing dark and the sound is other worldly. In between there are hundreds of other species in a given area, each broadcasting its call for a brief period each day.

Rainforest dwelling tribes, like the Penan of Borneo, are so adept at distinguishing these different calls, and the cicadas adhere to such strict scheduling, that the Penan use them to tell the time of day almost with the accuracy of a watch.

If you happen to have a small tape recorder try recording cicada songs for three seconds every 5-10 minutes. You will be amazed at the diversity when you play them back closer together. Another good activity is to see if you can actually locate a singing cicada. They are superbly camouflaged and stop singing abruptly when they sense danger.

Many birds, reptiles and small mammals prey on these succulent insects. In many parts of Southeast Asia people too consider these insects a choice delicacy. They are commonly eaten in Isan, Northeast Thailand.

CICADA LIFE CYCLE

19. LIANA VINES

Look overhead at the remarkable woody vines twisting their way through the lower canopy. Lianas have evolved an energy-efficient strategy for finding a place in the sun. Unlike trees, which spend much of their available energy slowly building supportive strength into their trunks, lianas are opportunistic climbers. They merely use trees for structural support.

In the early growth stages of many lianas, the growing tip of the vine is photophobic, i.e. it grows towards darkness rather than towards light as do most plants. This unique adaptation allows lianas to climb rapidly by continuously wrapping around any vertical, or horizontal, support base.

Even though their own stems may be only a few centimeters in diameter, lianas often have leaf systems as extensive as those of huge emergent trees whose bases can reach diameters in excess of four meters. Woody liana vines connect the trees of lowland tropical forests both vertically and horizontally. This makes for extremely dangerous conditions for logging. It is not uncommon for liana connected groups of trees to all come crashing down together when one emergent tree is cut or toppled by natural conditions.

Liana vines are important to forest-dwelling tribes throughout Southeast Asia. They serve as rope for lashing together simple dwellings, making packboards, baskets, fish traps, etc. Some lianas have natural water chambers – an important feature for nomadic peoples wandering far from creek sources. Some species have toxic latex saps which can be combined with certain add mixtures to make lethal poisons. Forest dwellers coat arrows and blow pipe darts with these mixtures for hunting. Liana poisons are also used to temporarily paralyze river fish – a major protein source obtained in an energy-efficient way. Some liana vines like the strangler fig, produce huge volumes of fruit which are eaten by humans, as well as animals which forest dwellers depend upon.

Malay tapir & young

20. NOCTURNAL ANIMALS & WILDLIFE TRACKS

Many visitors to tropical rainforests express disappointment at not seeing many of the larger animals that should be present. It is not surprising considering that most people are searching for wildlife at midday when you're least likely to see anything.

Animals here are extremely wary of humans as they have been preyed upon by forest dwellers for more than 50,000 years, and continue to be taken by poachers for food, pets and animal parts. The greatest deterrent to wildlife viewing, however, is the simple fact that the majority of larger animals found here are nocturnal by nature. All of the cats, bears, civets, deer, and even elephants, largely restrict their movements to hours of darkness. This strategy for survival may be designed to avoid the rnost dangerous predator on the planet – humans.

The key to wildlife tracks presented in this book is designed to give the day hiker a better understanding of what is moving about here in the dark. Look for tracks and scat along sandy or muddy river banks here or near wet sections of trails. A night walk, or a quiet blind, with occassional torch or hallogen lamp illumination can prove even more rewarding. Keep your group size extremely small, quiet, dressed in dark clothing and don't smoke. These tips will improve your chances of nocturnal sightings. Here's what is out there:

Tigers (Panthera tigris) are the most prized sightings at Khao Sok. They are also the least sighted. Tiger populations here are unknown, but the size of this national park and the adjacent wildlife santuaries make it one of the few viable tiger habitats in all of Thailand. Tracks and scat are sometimes seen along this trail system during certain times of the year, even though sightings are rare. The tiger is a good swimmer and hunts its prey by night. Wild boar and deer are the most common prey as they are most abundant, but tapir and other mammals are also taken. Tiger are the largest of all cats and can weigh 300 kilograms.

Statistically, tigers pose less danger to park visitors than falling over a waterfall or having a vehicle accident. Still they can be deadly, especially in defense of a kill site, or a mother with its young, or an old or wounded animal. Even though your chances of a tiger encounter are slight, use caution when hiking at night. Leopard, golden cat and clouded leopard are also present at Khao Sok but rarely seen. The small fishing cat, with its beautiful leopard-like markings, is a much more common sight along the riverbanks where it fishes by night. The Malay sun bear (Helarctos malayanus), Asiatic black bear (Ursus thibetanus) and Malay tapir (Topirus indicus) are other large nocturnal mammals occasionally seen along this trail. A much more likely sighting is the bush-tailed porcupine and the giant common porcupine, which is the size of a medium dog. Like many nocturnal creatures, these long-quilled mammals are commonly sighted in the early morning and evening hours as well as by night.

Most of the ungulates at Khao Sok have also adopted nocturnal strategies. The largest member of the deer family found here is the sambar deer (Cerrus unicolor), a favourite prey of tiger. Sambar bucks grow antlers with three branches once fully mature, and they shed these each November. You may see their antlers lying in the forest even if you don't spot the deer.

The barking deer (Muntiacus muntjack) is much smaller than the sambar and is largely preyed upon by leopard. Barking deer can be seen either by day or night feeding on young bamboo and grass shoots. This unusual deer has a fang which serves as a defense weapon. It also emits a distinct barking sound, hence its name. The bucks of this species shed their antlers annually.

The diminutive lesser mouse deer (Tragulusjavanicus) is the size of a small dog and one of the world's smallest hoofed animals. Its hoof prints are the size of your small fingernail. Quiet and timid, they are commonly seen near dusk and dawn, choosing to sleep out the heat of the day in deep forest refuge.

There are two species of wild oxen found at Khao Sok: the gaur (Bos gaurus) and the banteng (Bos javanicus). Both species forage by night on young leaves, shoots, and grasses, frequently alongside wild pig, sambar and barking deer.

Yet another nocturnal resident of the park is the serow (Capricornis sumatraensis), a sort of goat-antelope. Shy and reclusive by nature, these ungulates have short bodies but long legs. They are extremely difficult to see as they typically inhabit steep limestone cliff faces along karsts. They seek shelter in deep brush by day and come out of hiding to feed starting at dusk.

There are two nocturnal mammals which visitors on a night safari are most likely to see along this trail: the palm civet and the slow loris. (See Tracks pgs. 157 - 158)

Civets are Old-World members of the mongoose family that are largely arboreal feeders. Fruit, eggs, frogs and small vertebraes make up the diet of these cat-like mammals. With a head like a fox and a mask like a raccoon, the palm civet is a most intriguing animal. It lacks a voice, communicating instead through scent glands whose secretions are prized as a perfume and medicine. Far less appealing are the civets anal glands which squirt a highly offensive odor at attackers much like a skunk. It is common to smell civet along this trail even if you don't see them.

The slow loris, or night monkey as it is sometimes called, is one of the most delighfful sightings on a night safari.

Well-furred, slow moving, and with large (night vision) eyes, it has the quaint, cuddly appearance of a stuffed toy. Fur colors vary from reddish brown to pale grey but all have a dark colored ring around each eye which adds emphasis to their size. A dark stripe runs down the spine to a short tail which is well hidden under the fur.

The slow loris (Nycticebus coucang) is related to the monkey but displays none of their hyper-activity level. Instead, it is ploddingly slow and methodical in its nightly search of food, largely fruit and flowers, but also large insects and small vertebrates. The Penan tribes people of Borneo say that when a slow loris comes upon a piece of green rattan fruit, it will hold it in both hands and stare at it until it ripens.

Don't let this mammal's apparent lethargy fool you. The slow loris can reach out and grab an insect with amazing speed. They do this with both hands while clutching a branch with their feet.

Slow loris

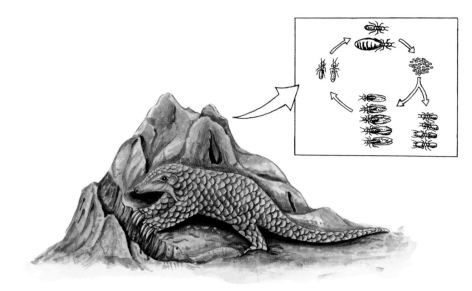

21. TERMITE MOUNDS

This medium sized termite mound is the home of a colony of macrotermes. These social insects do not feed on wood as is commonly believed, as they lack enzymes in their gut to break down wood cellulose. Rather, they have created here a dark and humid fungus-growing chamber where they cultivate fungus gardens for their food.

Termites must reproduce prolifically and constantly create new nest chambers as they are heavily preyed upon by other insects, reptiles, birds, and even large mammals.

The Malay pangolin or scaly anteater (Manis javanica) is a notorious excavator of termite and ant mounds. Resembling a reptile with its body armor of large scales this mammal has powerful claws for digging and a very long sticky tongue (up to 40 cm) for scooping up ants and termites. When threatened by a predator the shy pangolin curls up into a tight ball to protect its scaleless underbelly. *(See photo, page 54)*

Even more formidable predators of termite mounds are the Malay sun bear and Asiatic black bear. Further along the trail you will note large excavations where bear have dug out entire colonies of termites.

Macrotermes is but one of many species of termites which display remarkable division of labor. Unlike ants and bees where the workers and soldiers are all of one sex, with termites they may be either sex, but only one male and one female in the entire colony reproduce.

The queen with her grossly-extended abdomen is little more than an egg laying machine, while the king has the role of fertilizing eggs at intervals. Both must be tended and fed by the workers. Workers carry out the important tasks of building and maintaining the nest chamber, the complex tunnels leading to it, and keeping it well supplied with wood fiber for the fungus gardens. Soldier termites, with greatly enlarged mouth parts, have the unenviable job of defending the nest chamber from enemies like pangolin and bear.

At certain times and seasons (often at dusk during the rainy season), the nest will send out great swarms of winged alates, male and female offspring, which fly off to establish new colonies. The great majority of alates perish, gorged on by dragonflies, lizards and insectivorous birds and bats. It only takes two survivors, however, one male and one female, to become the king and queen of a new colony.

22. ANIMAL EXCAVATIONS

It you have been observant along the trail you may have already noticed extensive ground disturbance and excavations in some areas.

The shallow trenching alongside the trail is usually the work of the common wild pig (Sus scrofa), digging with their tusks and snouts for roots, tubers, worms and grubs. Even shallower scratching is the work of the red jungle fowl (Gallus gallus), scattering leaf litter and surface soil in search of insects and seed. Few people realize that the domestic chicken and pig, now distributed world-wide, have their origins here in the Southeast Asian rainforest. In fact the average domestic chicken is not much different from its wild cousin. If you hear crowing here early in the morning, it's the jungle fowl cock proclaiming his territory. (See photo, page 98)

The large excavations you see at this site are not the work of wild pigs, and certainly not that of jungle fowl. It is rather the deep diggings of a Malay sun bear or the Asiatic black bear, feasting on an excavated termite colony.

Both species of bear are found at Khao Sok though the Malay sun bear is much more common. As both species are largely nocturnal, it is unlikely you will encounter one in daylight.

The Malay sun bear, also known as the honey bear, is the world's smallest bear, but pound for pound, may be the most powerful. They have a handsome white cresent across the chest of their short-fur black coat, exceptionally long tongues for reaching bee larvae, honey and termites, and very long claws for digging and tearing. The sun bear is a good climber and can tear open a bee hive in a hardwood tree chamber with such devastating force, it looks as though a charge of dynamite has been detonated.

Neither the sun bear, nor the Asiatic black bear hibernate, but roam the forest year round. Don't be fooled by the sun bear's small size or teddy bear cuteness.

If you should encounter one of these bear – back off, they can be dangerous, especially females with cubs. They are the best climbers of all bear species so don't even think about going up a tree for safety.

As already mentioned, the scaly anteater, or pangolin, is another excavator, though diggings tend to be less extensive than those of bears.

There are other deep excavations you may occasionally come across– especially on the ridge trail to the rafflesia. These could only be the work of the tool using species, Homo sapiens, mining for tin in the 1970s and 80s.

23. WINGED SEEDS & LEGUMES

Although the Southeast Asian rain-forest boasts more than 100 different plant families with several thousand tree species there are two main families that predominate: those with double winged seeds (Dipterocarpaceae) and the legumes (Leguminosae).
Look for these different seeds on the

tetonic plates about 30 million years ago when the India subcontinent collided with continental Asia, infiltrating what is now Southeast Asia with new species. The dipterocarps were so successful at colonizing this new realm that they quickly became the dominate species. Mixed dipterocarps are the grandest fea-

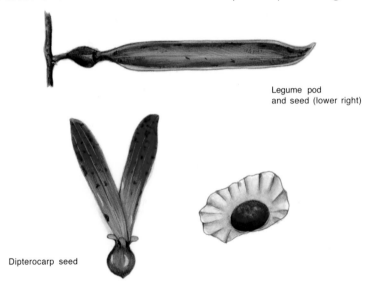

Legume pod
and seed (lower right)

Dipterocarp seed

ground here and all along the trail. Note how many seed types are dependent on wind dispersal as their parent trees rise so high above the canopy.
It is interesting that some of the biggest trees in this forest belong to plant families that grow in temperate latitudes as small bushes or annual herbs such as trees of the bean family (Leguminosae) and the violet family (Violacece).
Dipterocarps, on the other hand, are restricted to the tropics. They may have arrived in this region aboard shifting

ture of this forest, representing the tallest, oldest and most massive trees found here. Many canopy dwellers feed and habitate in these trees, and hornbills seek out dipterocarps as their preferred nest sites.
Dipterocarps must be 50-60 years old before they produce their first flowers and fruit; thereafter they only fruit every eight or nine years. At such times, wildlife populations may increase dramatically to take advantage of the sudden bounty of fruit. Dipterocarps are

very valuable to humans as well. It is common near settlements to see square holes chopped into the base of dipterocarps where villagers light small fires to stimulate the flow of sap. The fragrant pitch of these trees is a superb caulking compound for boat hulls. Unfortunately, the most outstanding feature of the giant dipterocarps is also their greatest downfall. Their beautiful, durable, straight-grained hardwood is highly coveted by six billion Homo sapiens. They are the object of intense desire by the logging industry, and tree poachers.

24. THE FOREST FLOOR

Tropical rainforests have been described as immensely sophisticated castles built on a foundation of sand. For unlike the nutrient-rich soils of temperate forests, most tropical forest soils are impoverished.

Tropical and temperate rainforests are, in some respects, opposite ecosystems. Temperate forests hold 80% of their nutrient base in the soil and it's here that the majority of life in these forests is found. Tropical forests, on the other hand, retain 80% of their nutrient base in the canopy, and it is here that half of all species on Earth can be found.

One reason for this reverse nutrient base in tropical forests is the phenomenal rate of decomposition of organic matter that falls to the forest floor. In one year six to eight tons of litter (leaves, seeds, fruit, bark, branches and trunks) will fall on an average hectare of Southeast Asian forest; yet this litter layer is only a few leaves deep at any given time. Scientists now tend to believe that fallen leaves don't have time to break down into organic top soil, but rather have their nutrients re-absorbed by tiny tree rootlets as they decompose.

If you look closely at the forest floor here you will see nutrient-deficient soil covered in an intricate web of rootlets and leaf litter. Tropical heat, and high humidity aid bacteria in the rapid recycling of these nutrients which are absorbed by the rootlets and carried through the living layer of the trunk, the cambium, back to the canopy. You are looking at the world's most efficient and advanced recycling system. Large limbs and fallen trees throughout this forest are being broken down by a host of decomposers, not the least of which are termites and fungi. There are more than 3,000 species of fungi in Thailand's forest and the infinite variations in form, color and texture of these fruiting bodies are among the most interesting features along this trail. Try not to disturb them as they are hard at work recycling, and others will enjoy seeing them too.

25. GIBBON CALLS

Just as the howl of the wolf has come to symbolize wilderness in temperate latitudes, so too does the song of the gibbon epitomize the last wild expanses of forest in Southeast Asia.

Take a moment here to listen to the calls of a family of gibbons across the river. If it is morning, between 8:00 and 10:00 am, then more than likely you will hear their songs. Gibbons are restricted to the Southeast Asian tropical forests. Of the nine species found here, it is the white handed or lar gibbon which is prevalent at Khao Sok. The lar (Hylobates lar) has two coat colorations: chocolate brown and creamy blond, with the darker being the genetically dominant characteristic. Regardless of coat color, all lar gibbons have a handsome tuft of white fur ringing a dark face and white hands and feet – hence their name.

The lar is light, swift, and wonderful to watch as it bracchiates (swings arm over arm) through the trees with the greatest of ease. The lar is so light it can work its way out to the far reaches of tree limbs in search of fruit, and is capable of tremendous leaps in moving from one tree to another.

Gibbons love pulpy ripe fruit but are known to eat leaves and the occasional insect or invertebrates. Because fruit is the mainstay of their diet, however, they must range widely (several km per day) to supply themselves. They also must defend their feeding territories vigorously – no simple task when a single family needs between 20 and 55 hectares. Ranges rarely overlap because they are so effectively defended, not by force, but by song. Gibbons, while no longer believed to be strictly monogamous, do often form mated bonds for life. They are also perhaps the most tuneful of all land mammals with each species charac-terized by its own unique song. Male and female gibbons protect their range and reinforce their pair bonds by singing duets each moring. Dueting is only done by largely monogamous species of birds and mammals.

The first gibbon calls of the day are usually solo performances of adult, or subadult males; later come the duets of mated pairs. Male and females have different parts which usually last 10 to 15 minutes.

Lar gibbon

The female lar gibbon has one of the greatest calls in all the animal kingdom. Believed to be a territorial warning to other females (basically: "I've got my male, keep back bitch!"), she works her way into a rising frenzy, then releases an almost hysterical scream that slowly fades to soft "Whoo-Whoo's". This is known as the "great call" and only bonded female gibbons in the wild seem capable of this dramatic vocalization. The duet calls of mated gibbons are unqiuely their own and improve the longer they live together.

When reflecting on the haunting beauty of gibbon songs it is easy to conjure up images of another mammal which has mastered song – the whale. Indeed there is a similarity here, not so much in the songs but the way in which they are broadcast. Just as whales use thermal boundaries where warm and cold currents meet to send their songs hundreds of kilometers across the ocean, so too does the gibbon take advantage of thermal boundaries in the rainforest canopy.

Gibbons sleep in the high emergent trees so they are in prime position to transmit their morning songs. The rising tropical sun heats the upper canopy much sooner than the understory and when the cool night air trapped under the foliage meets the hot air of the sun drenched upper canopy, a thermal boundary is created. By timing their calls to coincide with this boundary, gibbons are able to project their songs 2-3 kilometers – much further than their voices would otherwise carry.

After the morning duets in the emergent trees, gibbons drop to the upper canopy to forage and travel where the foliage is more continuous. They usually return to a tall tree to rest, groom and play during the middle of the day. Mated pairs usually have one or more offspring in the family. Average group size is four and only ranges from 2-6. Grooming the fur for lice, ticks and forest debris keeps wild gibbons both clean and closely bonded. They certainly look well-groomed compared to their pathetic kin held captive as pets throughout Thailand.

Other than large eagles and pythons, the gibbon has few predators to fear with one notable exception – humans. National parks and wildlife sanctuaries are virtually the only places in Thailand where gibbons remain in the wild, yet they are under intense poaching pressure. Every baby gibbon you see as a pet in Thailand means that the mother was shot to get it and an entire monogamous family unit was torn apart. So much of a gibbons foraging skills and social behavior is learned from their parents that it is extremely difficult, if not completely impossible, to reintroduce these orphans back into the wild.

Gibbon have very low reproductive rates and populations will not survive long into this century unless this illegal trade is seriously curtailed. Gibbons are much more than a symbol of the wild, they and hornbills are keystone species playing important roles in seed dispersal. They are also among the first species to disappear when the forest is too impacted. The wildlife symphony of the Khao Sok rainforest would certainly be sadder and quieter without them.

26. BUTTRESSED ROOTS

One of the most striking features of tropical rainforests are the dramatically enlarged root bases of certain trees. While members of the fig family (ficus) are exemplary in these developments, they are not alone. Many, but not all, emergent trees, those that rise above the upper canopy, develop these wide buttressed roots as a result of the vertical development of the principal lateral roots.

Botanists offer various explanations for these adaptations :

1)	Emergent trees rising high above the general canopy are subjected to intense winds during tropical storms, yet they have dangerously shallow root systems. There is abundant water near the surface so the tree has no need to send down deep tap roots. Instead, root systems of large trees are often partially exposed, spreading wide and shallow rather than deep since nutrients are concentrated only near the surface. The buttressing is simply a means of holding the huge trees upright, much like the base of a Gothic column.

temperate rainforests along the Pacific Coast of North American produce trees that are much taller, of greater girth and older than those of tropical rainforests. There is even more biomass, i.e. weight of living matter, in the temperate rainforest than the tropical.

The category where tropical rainforests win hands down, however, is in their extraordinary biodiversity. The rainforest you see before you may have more than 200 species of trees per hectare. A temperate rain-forest, by contrast, would be

considered exceptionally diverse to have ten tree species per hectare.

2)	Another, or further, explanation of this feature is that flared roots greatly expand the surface area of the bark at the base of the tree – the living cambium tissue that is so essential to the flow of water and nutrients to the massive foilage in the canopy.

The tallest trunks of the largest tropical rainforest trees may rise 30 meters from their base to the first branch with the top of the trees crown extending more than 65 meters above the ground. Impressive as they are, trees of this stature are never more than 150-300 years old. Many people are surprised to learn that

Flared root bases not only serve their tree well, but have utilitarian uses for humans. Local villagers and forest-dwelling tribes fashion boat prows from them. The Asmat in western New Guinea make war shields from them and tribes people from Borneo to the Amazon use then for drums to communicate locations. By thumping the foot against one of the large thin folds, a deep sound resonates that carries through the forest further than a human voice. This style of communication is also less likely to frighten prey species when hunting.

27. LEECH LIFE CYCLE

Perhaps by now you too are a living part of this rainforest ecosystem – even if not by choice. No, you haven't been eaten by a tiger, swallowed by a python, or picked to pieces by hungry ants, but more than likely you've provided a meal for a hungry leech. Check your ankles and feet, especially if it has recently rained.

Leeches are amazing creatures that have probably been around as long as the forest itself (approx 160 million years) and in spite of human loathing, will likely be around long after us. These simple but successful parasites wait out dry periods under wet leaf litter then emerge when animal trails are wet. Leeches are attracted by movement, warmth, and carbon dioxide levels in the air a sure sign that a bird or mammal is nearby.

Leaf leeches or tiger leeches (Haemadipsa picta) have a painful bite,

but fortunately, neither they nor water leeches are found at Khao Sok. The Common leech (Haemadipsa zeylanica) that is found here is relatively benign. It awaits the passage of prey along trails frequented by mammals – humans included.

Leeches have suckers at each end of the body, but only one mouth part with three saw-like teeth. After penetrating the skin with these teeth, the leech injects an extremely efficient anticoagulant which makes the blood letting appear far more serious than the tiny surgical wound should warrant.

The feeding leech absorbs several times its own body weight in blood before dropping off. One meal may last for six months or more. Leeches satiated with blood are largely immobile and become easy prey for foraging birds like the red jungle fowl (Gallus gallus) or the great

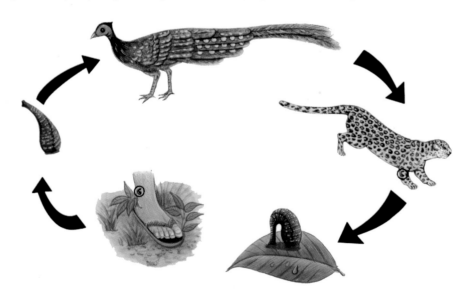

argus pheasant (Argusianus argus)– both common residents at Khao Sok. The birds in turn, may fall prey to a jungle cat or leopard later that night. These cats themselves may serve as prey for new leeches. Thus your few drops of blood quickly become part of the oldest living ecosystem on Earth.

Leech bites are greatly exaggerated in popular folklore. There is no real danger at all. You can easily remove a leech by gently easing it off with a fingernail. Though leech wounds will bleed a bit, and may itch afterwards, they do not infect unless excessively scratched.

Leeches are still vital to successful surgery when fingers are grafted back onto a hand ; they are used to stimulate the flow of blood to the re-grafted appendage.

Tobacco is considered a good leech deterrent when stuffed in the rim of your socks. Certain insect repellents are also effective until water and sweat wash them away. The pig-tail macaque, (Macaca nemestrina) a powerfully-built baboon-like monkey found here at Khao Sok, may have the best defense strategy of all. This is the only forest monkey that prefers to rest on the ground and as leeches come crawling towards the macaques they simply pick them off and eat them. Try it, they're pure protein.

If preying on a parasite isn't to your liking try befriending a leech instead. People who keep leeches as pets claim they are the best pets of all. They require little space, make great traveling companions, bond closely with their owner and only need one small feeding from your finger every 6-12 months to stay healthy and happy.

If you are treking this trail in the rainy season leeches may become your preoccupation. (A park officer here boasts a record of 186 leeches during an 8 km hike.) Rather than let leeches spoil your experience try a little game with your hiking companions. The Khao Sok point system is simple to follow attatched leech = 1 point; drawn blood 2 points; fed & escaped = 5 points; inside undershorts = 10 points. Whoever scores highest gets treated to drinks (Bloody Mary's) back at your bungalow by your hiking partners.

28. CAULIFLORY & BAT POLLINATION

Cauliflory is the name given to the unusual fruit clusters that grow from the trunk and sides of stems of many tropical forest trees and lianas. While no one knows for certain what purpose this evolutionary adaptation serves, there is speculation that it may aid some plants in the pollination of flowers and fruit dispersal by bats. Rather than having to negotiate the dense maze of vegetation in the canopy, bats can easily find their way to these clusters of flowers and fruit along the trunks.

Cauliflory is not the only strategy plants use to attract pollinators. Many rainforest trees bloom only at night to attract bats and a menagerie of other nocturnal nectar sippers.

There are 92 species of bats in Thailand and they are critical to the maintenance of healthy forest ecosystems. Some bat species are insectivorous, consuming billions of insects (pests) that feed on forest vegetation, every night. They also help control the number of mosquitoes and biting flies that prey on birds and mammals.

Some species of bats are nectar sippers, and in many cases are the sole pollinators of rainforest flowers. Still others, like the giant fruit bat, or "flying fox" are frugivores, gorging on the cornicopia of pulpy ripe fruits and widely dispersing their seeds.

All bat species directly benefit epiphytic plants in the rainforest canopy through their nitiogen-rich feces. Judging by the depth of bat guano in nearby caves, literally tons of fertilizer must be dropped each night over the canopy during their feeding forays.

It is interesting to note that of the approximately 4,000 species of mammals in the world about 900 of them are bats. That's a huge proportion. It may be comforting to also note that of these 900 species only three are vampire species and none of the vampire species are found here.

29. FIGS & FIG WASPS

This short side trail leads 100 meters to the base of a huge fig tree which is one of the most prolific producers of fruit in the forest. If the tree is in fruit you should see any number of animals feeding here: hornbills, gibbons, wild boar, deer, macaques, tapir, bear, civet, squirrel, slow loris, bats and many fruit-eating birds. (Note: The crown of this same tree is visible by looking up-river when crossing the bridge to the next and last marker.)

and fragility of tropical forest ecosystems. Consider, for example, that of the hundreds of species of figs each has a single species of fig wasp responsible for pollination. This is a remarkable example of co-evolution and one of the very few rainforest mysteries science now has some knowledge of.

The fruit of the fig is not really a fruit at all, but a chamber-like pseudo fruit, the inside of which is lined with tiny flowers. The only entrance to the chamber is at the base of the fruit which is covered by

There are nearly 400 fig species in Thailand alone and many more in the Indo-Malayan realm. It is hard to imagine a more important food source for forest dwelling animals living both in the canopy and on the ground ; yet none of this would be possible without a tiny insect.

The species Ficus epitomizes the incredible complexity, interrelatedness,

tiny scales. It is through this entrance that the female fig wasp forces her way inside to take her chance at reproduction. It is purely a matter of chance because once inside there is no escape, yet not all figs have gall flowers necessary for reproduction. If the fig has only female flowers, these will be fertilized by the pollen the female wasp carries from the fig fruit in which she was hatched. Unfortunately for the wasp, the long style of the female flowers prevent her from depositing her eggs. The wasp will die, trapped within the flower she pollinated but with no chance of reproduction herself.

If, however, the fig has gall flowers, the female can lay her eggs and a new generation of fig wasps, both male and female, will hatch within the chamber. The newly-hatched females mate with the wingless males and, dusted in pollen from the mating ritual, break out of the fig chamber as it ripens and begins to decompose. The males die inside the fig, never having seen the outside world, while the females, fertilized and laden with pollen emerge in great swarms of insects above the fig trees to search out new fruit and begin the cycle all over again.

Before returning to the main trail to complete the last station of this Interpretive Trail, check the ground here for fallen figs. Break open a few and you will have a first-hand illustration of this lesson.

30. AQUATIC ECOSYSTEMS

You have now crossed onto a small island in the Sok River which is the end of the Interpretive Trail. Take some time here to rest and explore this amazing aquatic ecosystem.

Fallen leaves and fruit form the basis of the nutrient economy of rainforest aquatic ecosystems. Many species of fish feed on fruit which drops from the canopy overhead or washes into waterways during torrential rainstorms.

Fallen leaves float down river until they settle to the bottom where aquatic insects and fresh water crustaceans aid in their decomposition. These species in turn provide protein-rich food for a variety of fish. There may be 30-40 fresh water fish species in these tributaries and they are preyed upon by just about everything.

Several species of kingfishers hunt their prey from overhanging branches. Watch for the metallic blue flash of plummage and bright beaks as they dart from perch to perch.

The little heon is camouflaged to match the creek boulders where it waits motionless to ambush its prey. Another bird to watch for here is the lesser fish eagle which conceals itself in over-hanging branches, then swoops down suddenly to snatch unsuspecting fish from the surface of deep river pools.

Several species of otter, with their swift and sleek bodies, occupy these waterways from river mouth to headwaters, feeding on small fish, tadpoles, molluscs and crustaceans.

The common water monitor lizard (Varanus salvator), which can attain lengths in excess of 2 meters, is another superbly adapted predator; it is equally adept at hunting fish and frogs in the water, or birds, eggs and small mammals on land.

Many species of frogs, turtles and snakes thrive in association with these fresh-water ecosystems. The Indo-chinese rat snake (Ptyas korros) with its long dark grey and incredibly swift body, can sometimes be seen patroling the shoreline in pursuit of rodents ; while the smaller red necked keelback (Rhabdophis subminiatus) with its handsome olive green body and red neck preys largely on frogs.

The world's largest or second largest snake (still open to debate) is also found here. The Asian reticulated python (Python reticulatus) with its dramatic and beautiful skin pattern can attain lengths in excess of 10 meters. Like the Anaconda of the Amazon it loves water and periodically soaks its body in quiet river pools. It is a superb swimmer and a powerful constrictor that literally crushes its prey before swallowing it whole. Wild boar, deer, gibbons, small jungle cats, and (at times) humans form the diet of the larger specimens. Though it is non-venomous, the python is unpredictable, incredibly powerful and generally feared. The Thais say that if a python's head is as large as your foot it can swallow you. Pythons prefer dark cool caves for resting and hunt their prey largely by night.

Other nocturnal visitors to these shores include the large and elusive Malayan tapir, which grazes on streamside vegetation and soaks in river pools, and wild boar, which root along stream banks for tubers, fallen fruit, worms and grubs. The principal predator of these large mammals, the tiger, is another occassional night time visitor here, as is the small fishing cat which snatches unwary fish with its sharp claws and teeth. Look for fishing cat tracks along the sand and mud banks. They are much more common than tiger tracks.

Elephants come here at night to graze on the rich elephant grass, the lush bamboo groves, the abundance of wild banana, and the "elephant apple" growing profusely on trees along the outer edge of this small island. Note the incredibly gnarled appearance of these trees, bruised and bending down river from decades of cascading logs and boulders which strike against them during the river's flood months (July - October).

During the early morning and evening, several species of macaque monkey come to feed by the riverside where fruit grows profusely in the abundant sunlight. Unlike gibbons and leaf monkeys which will not cross any body of water, the long-tailed macaques are rather fond of it. They are good swimmers and love to eat fresh water molluscs, prawn, crab and any other protein they can forage from the river's edge.

During the day it is common to see large swarms of brilliant butterflies gathering along sandy or muddy riverbanks where mammals have recently urinated. Irridescent green and red damselflies and the larger dragon flies are other common sights. The males are extremely territorial and you may see them defending air space above quiet back eddies in the river, or mating in flight with a female. The female is often observed dipping her abdomen to the waters surface as she ovideposits her eggs for a new generation.

Water spiders dart across the water surface to quickly snatch any insect that is carried down from the canopy on falling leaves. Tadpoles graze algae on the rocks and fish dart about in search of their preferred prey. There is literally life on top of life here, just as there is in the forest at large.

Don't be disappointed if at first you don't see much, because most large animals come here only by night. Marvel in the little creatures instead : the frogs, tadpoles, turtles, snakes, lizards and the amazing diversity of insects and fish. Look for wildlife tracks along the sand bars and mud banks. Above all, take in the sounds, the smells, and the serenity of this place. It is part of the oldest living terrestrial ecosystem on Earth, and at this very moment, the simple exchange of your breath makes you and it a part of each other.

SPECIES LIST

A) BIRD SPECIES (EXPECTED / CONFIRMED) FROM KHAO SOK

Scientific Name	English Name	Scientific Name	English Name
☐ Tachybaptus ruficollis	Little Grebe	☐ Rollulus rouloul	Crested Wood-Partridge
☐ Butorides striatus	Little Heron	☐ Lophura ignita	Crested Fireback
☐ Ardeola bacchus	Chinese Pond Heron	☐ Gallus gallus	Red Jungle Fowl
☐ Bubulcus ibis	Cattle Egret	☐ Polyplectron malacense	Malayan Peacock Pheasant
☐ Egretta intermedia	Intermediate Egret	☐ Argusianus argus	Great Argus Pheasant
☐ Egretta garzetta	Little Egret	☐ Turnix suscitator	Barred Buttonquail
☐ Gorsachius melanolophus	Malayan Night-Heron	☐ Rallus striatus	Slaty-breasted Rail
☐ Ixobrychus sinensis	Yellow Bittern	☐ Rallina fasciata	Red-legged Crake
☐ Ixobrychus eurhythmus	Schrenck's Bittern	☐ Rallina eurizonoides	Slaty-legged Crake
☐ Ixobrychus cinnamomeus	Cinnamon Bittern	☐ Porzana fusca	Ruddy-breasted Crake
☐ Dupetor flavicollis	Black Bittern	☐ Amaurornis phoenicurus	White-breasted Watercock
☐ Mycteria leucocephala	Painted Stork	☐ Gallicrex cinerea	Watercock
☐ Ciconia episcopus	Woolly-necked Stork	☐ Heliopais personata	Masked Finfoot
☐ Ciconia stormi	Storm's Stork	☐ Metopidius indicus	Bronze-winged Jacana
☐ Dendrocygna javanica	Lesser Whistling Duck	☐ Rostratula benghalensis	Greater Painted Snip
☐ Cairina scutulata	White-winged Duck	☐ Vanellus indicus	Red-wattled Lapwing
☐ Pandion haliaetus	Osprey	☐ Vanellus duvaucelii	River Lapwing
☐ Aviceda jerdoni	Jerdon's Baza	☐ Charadrius dubius	Little Ringed Plover
☐ Aviceda leuphotes	Black Baza	☐ Numemius phaeopus	Whimbrel
☐ Pernis ptilorhyncus	Crested Honey-Buzzard	☐ Tringa glareola	Wood Sandpiper
☐ Macheiramphus alcinus	Bat Hawk	☐ Gallinago stenura	Pintail Snipe
☐ Elanus caeruleus	Black-shouldered Kite	☐ Scolopax rusticola	Eurasian Woodcock
☐ Milvus migrans	Black Kite	☐ Treron curvirostra	Thick-billed Pigeon
☐ Haliastur indus	Brahminy Kite	☐ Treron olax	Little Green Pigeon
☐ Haliaeetus leucogaster	White-bellied Sea-Eagle	☐ Treron vernans	Pink-necked Pigeon
☐ Ichthyophage humilis	Lesser Fish-Eagle	☐ Treron bicincta	Orange-breasted Pigeon
☐ Ichthyophage ichthyaetus	Grey-headed Fish-Eagle	☐ Treron capellei	Large Green Pigeon
☐ Spilornis cheela	Crested Serpent-Eagle	☐ Ducula aenea	Green Imperial Pigeon
☐ Circus spilonotus	Eastern Marsh Harrie	☐ Ducula bicolor	Pied Imperial Pigeon
☐ Accipiter gularis	Japanese Sparrowhawk	☐ Columba livia	Rock Pigeon
☐ Accipiter trivirgatus	Crested Goshawk	☐ Streptopelia chinensis	Spotted Dove
☐ Accipiter soloensis	Chinese Goshawk	☐ Geopelia striata	Zebra Dove
☐ Accipiter badius	Shikra	☐ Chalcophaps indica	Emerald Dove
☐ Butastur indicus	Grey-faced Buzzard	☐ Psittinus cyanurus	Blue-rumped Parrot
☐ Ictinaetus malayensis	Black Eagle	☐ Loriculus vernailis	Vernal Hanging Parrot
☐ Hieraaetus Kienerii	Rufous-bellied Eagle	☐ Cuculus sparverioides	Large Hawk-Cuckoo
☐ Spizaetus cirrhatus	Changable Hawk-Eagle	☐ Cuculus vagans	Moustached Hawk Cuckoo
☐ Spizaetus nipalensis	Mountain Hawk-Eagle	☐ Cuculus fugax	Hodgson's Hawk Cuckoo
☐ Spizaetus alboniger	Blyth's Hawk-Eagle	☐ Cuculus micropterus	Indian Cuckoo
☐ Spizaetus nanus	Wallace's Hawk-Eagle	☐ Cuculus saturatus	Oriental Cuckoo
☐ Microhierax fringillarius	Black-thighed Falconet	☐ Cacomantis sonneratii	Banded Bay Cuckoo
☐ Falco tinnunculus	Eurasian Kestrel	☐ Cacomantis merulinus	Plaintive Cuckoo
☐ Falco severus	Oriental Hobby	☐ Cacomantis sepulcralis	Rusty-breasted Cuckoo
☐ Falco peregrinus	Peregrine Falcon	☐ Chrysococcyx maculatus	Asian Emerald Cuckoo
☐ Rhizothera longirostris	Long-billed Partridge	☐ Chrysococcyx xanthorhynch	Violet Cuckoo
☐ Coturnix chinensis	Blue-breasted Quail	☐ Surniculus lugubris	Drongo Cuckoo
☐ Arborophila charltonii	Scaly-breasted Partridge	☐ Eudynamys scolopacea	Common Koel
☐ Caloperdix oculea	Ferruginous Wood-Partidge	☐ Phaenicophaeus diardi	Black-bellied Malkoha

Scientific Name	English Name	Scientific Name	English Name
☐ Phaenicophaeus sumatranus	Chesnut-bellied Malkoha	☐ Anorrhinus galeritus	Bushy-crested Hornbill
☐ Phaenicophaeus tristis	Green-billed Malkoha	☐ Rhyticeros corrugatus	Wrinkled Hornbill
☐ Phaenicophaeus chlorophae	Raffles's Malkoha	☐ Rhyticeros undulatus	Wreathed Hornbill
☐ Phaenicophaeus javanicus	Red-billed Malkoha	☐ Anthracoceros malayanus	Black Hornbill
☐ Phaenicophaeus curvirostr	Chestnut breasted Malkoha	☐ Anthracoceros albirostris	Pied Hornbill
☐ Centropus sinensis	Greater Coucal	☐ Buceros bicornis	Great Hornbill
☐ Centropus bengalensis	Lesser Coucal	☐ Rhinoplax vigil	Helmeted Hornbill
☐ Tyto alba	Barn Owl	☐ Megalaima lineata	Lineated Barbet
☐ Phodilus badius	Bay Owl	☐ Megalaima chrysopogon	Gold-whiskered Barbet
☐ Otus sagittatus	White-fronted Scops Owl	☐ Megalaima rafflesii	Red-crowned Barbet
☐ Otus lempiji	Collared Scops Owl	☐ Megalaima mystacophanos	Red-throated Barbet
☐ Bubo sumatranus	Barred Eagle Owl	☐ Megalaima australis	Blue-eared Barbet
☐ Ketupa ketupu	Buffy Fish Owl	☐ Megalaima haemacephala	Coppersmith Barbet
☐ Ninox scutulata	Brown Hawk Owl	☐ Calorhamphus fuliginosus	Brown Barbet
☐ Strix seloputo	Spotted Wood Owl	☐ Indicator archipelagicus	Malaysian Honeyguide
☐ Strix leptogrammica	Brown Wood Owl	☐ Sasia ochracea	White-browed Piculet
☐ Batrachostomus javensis	Javan Frogmouth	☐ Sasia abnormis	Rufous Piculet
☐ Eurostopodus macrotis	Great Eared Nightjar	☐ Celeus brachyurus	Rufous Woodpecker
☐ Caprimulgus macrotis	Large-tailed Nightjar	☐ Picoides atratus	Stripe-breasted Woodpecker
☐ Aerodramus fuciphagus	Edible-nest Swiftlet	☐ Picus puniceus	Crimson-winged Woodpecker
☐ Collocalia esculenta	White-bellied Swiftlet	☐ Picus mentalis	Checker-throated Woodpecker
☐ Hirundapus giganteus	Brown Needletail	☐ Picus miniaceus	Banded Woodpecker
☐ Rhaphidura leucopygialis	Silver-rumped Swift	☐ Dinopium javanense	Common Flameback
☐ Apus pacificus	Pacific Swift	☐ Dinopium rafflesii	Olive-backed Woodpecker
☐ Apus affinis	House Swift	☐ Gecinulus viridis	Bamboo Woodpecker
☐ Cypsiurus balasiensis	Asian Palm Swift	☐ Meiglyptes trists	Buff-rumped Woodpecker
☐ Hemiprocne longipennis	Grey-rumped Treeswift	☐ Meiglyptes tukki	Buff-necked Woodpecker
☐ Hemiprocne comata	Whiskered Treeswift	☐ Muelleripicus pulverulent	Great Slaty Woodpecker
☐ Harpactes kasumba	Red-naped Trogon	☐ Dryocopus javensis	White-bellied Woodpecker
☐ Harpactes orrhophaeus	Cinnamon-rumped Trogon	☐ Picoides canicapillus	Grey-capped Woodpecker
☐ Harpactes duvaucelii	Scarlet-rumped Trogon	☐ Hemicircus concretus	Grey-and-buff Woodpecker
☐ Harpactes oreskios	Orange-breasted Trogon	☐ Blythipicus rubiginosus	Maroon Woodpecker
☐ Alcedo atthis	Common Kingfisher	☐ Chrysocolaptes lucidus	Greater Flameback
☐ Alcedo meninting	Blue-eared Kingfisher	☐ Corydon sumatranus	Dusky Broadbill
☐ Alcedo euryzona	Blue-banded Kingfisher	☐ Cymbirhynchus macrorhynch	Black-and-red Broadbill
☐ Ceyx erithacus	Black-backed Kingfisher	☐ Eurylaimus javanicus	Banded Broadbill
☐ Ceyx rufidorsus	Rufous-backed Kingfisher	☐ Eurylaimus ochromalus	Black/yellow Broadbill
☐ Halcyon capensis	Stork-billed Kingfisher	☐ Calyptomena viridis	Green Broadbill
☐ Lacedo pulchella	Banded Kingfisher	☐ Pitta caerulea	Giant Pitta
☐ Halcyon coromanda	Ruddy Kingfisher	☐ Pitta moluccensis	Blue-winged Pitta
☐ Halcyon smyrnensis	White-throated Kingfisher	☐ Pitta sordida	Hooded Pitta
☐ Halcyon pileata	Black-capped Kingfisher	☐ Pitta cyanea	Blue Pitta
☐ Halcyon chloris	White-collared Kingfisher	☐ Pitta guajana	Banded Pitta
☐ Actenoides concretius	Rufous-collared Kingfisher	☐ Pitta gurneyi	Gurney's Pitta
☐ Merops leschenaulti	Chestnut-headed Bee Eater	☐ Riparia riparia	Sand Martin
☐ Merops philippinus	Blue-tailed Bee-Eater	☐ Hirundo concolor	Dusky Crag Martin
☐ Merops viridis	Blue-throated Bee-Eater	☐ Hirundo rustica	Barn Swallow
☐ Nyctyornis amictus	Red-bearded Bee-Eater	☐ Hirundo tahitica	Pacific Swallow
☐ Coracias benghalensis	Indian Roller	☐ Hirundo daurica	Red-rumped Swallow
☐ Eurystomus orientalis	Dollarbird	☐ Hemipus picatus	Bar-winged Flycatcher-shrike
☐ Upupa epops	Hoopoe	☐ Tephrodornis virgatus	Large Wood-shrike
☐ Buceros rhinoceros	Rhinocerous Hornbill	☐ Coracina melaschista	Black-winged Cuckoo-shrike
☐ Berenicornis comatus	White-crowned Hornbill	☐ Coracina fimbriata	Lesser Cuckoo-shrike

Scientific Name	English Name	Scientific Name	English Name
☐ Lalage nigra	Pied Triller	☐ Trichastoma abbotti	Abbott's Babbler
☐ Pericrocotus divaricatus	Ashy Minivet	☐ Malacopteron magnirostre	Moustached Babbler
☐ Pericrocotus roseus	Rosy Minivet	☐ Malacopteron affine	Sooty-capped Babbler
☐ Pericrocotus cinnamomeus	Small Minivet	☐ Malacopteron cinereum	Scaly-crowned Babbler
☐ Pericrocotus igneus	Fiery Minivet	☐ Malacopteron magnum	Rufous-crowned Babbler
☐ Pericrocotus flammeus	Scarlet Minivet	☐ Napothera macrodactyla	Large Wren-Babbler
☐ Aegithina viridissima	Green Iora	☐ Napothere brevicaudata	Streaked Wren-Babbler
☐ Aegithina tiphia	Common Iora	☐ Stachyris rufifrons	Rufous-fronted Babbler
☐ Aegithina lafresnayei	Great Iora	☐ Stachyris nigriceps	Grey-throated Babbler
☐ Chloropsis eyanopogon	Lesser Green Leafbird	☐ Stachyris poliocephala	Grey-headed Babbler
☐ Chloropsis sonnerati	Greater Green Leafbird	☐ Stachyris striolata	Spot-necked Babbler
☐ Chloropsis cochinchinensi	Blue-winged Leafbird	☐ Stachyris maculate	Chestnut-rumped Babbler
☐ Pycnonotus zeylanicus	Straw-headed Bulbul	☐ Stachyris nigricollis	Black-throated Babbler
☐ Pycnonotus atriceps	Black-headed Bulbul	☐ Stachyris erythroptera	Chestnut-winged Babbler
☐ Pycnonotus melanicterus	Black-crested Bulbul	☐ Macronous gularis	Striped Tit-Babbler
☐ Pycnonotus squamatus	Scaly-breasted Bulbul	☐ Macronous ptilosus	Fluffy-backed Tit-Babbler
☐ Pycnonotus cyaniventris	Grey-bellied Bulbul	☐ Alcippe poioicephala	Brown-cheeked Fulvetta
☐ Pycnonotus jocosus	Red-whiskered Bulbul	☐ Yuhina zantholeuca	White-bellied Yuhina
☐ Pycnonotus eutilotus	Puff-backed Bulbul	☐ Eupetes macrocerus	Malaysian Rail-Babbler
☐ Pycnonotus finlaysoni	Stripe-throated Bulbul	☐ Luscinia cyane	Siberian Blue Robin
☐ Pycnonotus goiavier	Yellow-vented Bulbul	☐ Copsychus saularis	Magpie Robin
☐ Pycnonotus plumosus	Olive-winged Bulbul	☐ Copsychus malabaricus	White-rumped Shama
☐ Pycnonotus blanfordi	Streak-eared Bulbul	☐ Enicurus ruficapillus	Chestnut-naped Forktail
☐ Pycnonotus simplex	Cream-vented Bulbul	☐ Enicurus leschenaulti	White-crowned Forktail
☐ Pycnonotus brunneus	Red-eyed Bulbul	☐ Saxicola torquata	Stonechat
☐ Pycnonotus erythropthalmo	Spectacled Bulbul	☐ Monticola gularis	White-throated Rock-Thrush
☐ Criniger ochraceus	Ochraceous Bulbul	☐ Monticola solitarius	Blue Rock-Thrush
☐ Criniger bres	Grey-cheeked Bulbul	☐ Myiophoneus caeruleus	Blue Whistling Thrush
☐ Criniger phaeocephalus	Yellow-bellied Bulbul	☐ Zoothera interpres	Chestnut-capped Thrush
☐ Hypsipetes criniger	Hairy-backed Bulbul	☐ Zoothera citrina	Orange-headed Thrush
☐ Hypsipetes charlottae	Buff-vented Bulbul	☐ Zoothera dauma	Scaly Thrush
☐ Hypsipetes malaccensis	Streaked Bulbul	☐ Turdus obscurus	Eye-browed Thrush
☐ Dicrurus macrocercus	Black Drongo	☐ Gerygone sulphurea	Flyeater
☐ Dicrurus leucophaeus	Ashy Drongo	☐ Abroscopus superciliaris	Yellow-bellied Warbler
☐ Dicrurus annectans	Crow-billed Drongo	☐ Phylloscopus inornatus	Inornate Warbler
☐ Dicrurus aeneus	Bronzed Drongo	☐ Phylloscopus borealis	Arctic Warbler
☐ Dicrurus paradiseus	Greater Racket-tailed Drongo	☐ Phylloscopus plumbeitarsu	Two-barred Warbler
☐ Oriolus xanthonotus	Dark-throated Oriole	☐ Phylloscopus tenellipes	Pale-legged Leaf Warbler
☐ Oriolus chinensis	Black-naped Oriole	☐ Phylloscopus coronatus	Eastern Crowned Warbler
☐ Oriolus xanthornus	Black-hooded Oriole	☐ Acrocephalus aedon	Thick-billed Warbler
☐ Irena puella	Asian Fairy Bluebird	☐ Acrocephalus arundinaceus	Great Reed-Warbler
☐ Platylophus galericulatus	Crested Jay	☐ Locustella lanceolata	Lanceolated Warbler
☐ Crypsirina temia	Racket-tailed Treepi	☐ Orthotomus sutorius	Common Tailorbird
☐ Platysmurus leucopterus	Black Magpie	☐ Orthotomus atrogularis	Dark-necked Tailorbird
☐ Corvus macrorhynchos	Large-billed Crow	☐ Orthotomus sericeus	Rufous-throated Tailorbird
☐ Melanochlora sultanea	Sultan Tit	☐ Prinia rufescens	Rufescent Prinia
☐ Sitta frontalis	Velvet fronted Nuthatch	☐ Prinia flaviventris	Yellow-bellied Prinia
☐ Pellorneum ruficeps	Puff-throated Babbler	☐ Cisticola juncidis	Zitting Cisticola
☐ Pellorneum capistratum	Black-capped Babbler	☐ Rhinomyias olivacea	Fulvous-chested Flycatcher
☐ Trichastoma tickelli	Buff-breasted Babbler	☐ Rhinomyias brunneata	Brown-chested Flycatcher
☐ Trichastoma malaccense	Short-tailed Babbler	☐ Muscicapa dauurica	Asian Brown Flycatcher
☐ Trichastoma rostratum	White-chested Babbler	☐ Muscicapa williamsoni	Brown-streaked Flycatcher
☐ Trichastoma bicolor	Ferruginous Babbler	☐ Muscicapa ferruginea	Ferruginous Flycatcher

Scientific Name	English Name	Scientific Name	English Name
Eumyias thalassina	Verditer Flycatcher	Cracula religiosa	Hill Myna
Ficedula zanthopygia	Yellow-rumped Flycatcher	Anthreptes simplex	Plain Sunbird
Ficedula mugimaki	Mugimaki Flycatcher	Anthreptes malacensis	Brown-throated Sunbird
Ficedula parva	Red-throated Flycatcher	Anthreptes rhodolaema	Red-throated Sunbird
Ficedula dumetoria	Rufous-chested Flycatcher	Anthreptes singalensis	Ruby-cheeked Sunbird
Cyanoptila cyanomelana	Blue-and-white Flycatcher	Hypogramma hypogrammicum	Purple-naped Sunbird
Cyornis banyumas	Hill Blue Flycatcher	Nectarinia sperata	Purple-throated Sunbird
Cyornis tickelliae	Tickell's Blue Flycatcher	Nectarinia jugularis	Olive-backed Sunbird
Culicicapa ceylonensis	Grey-headed Flycatcher	Aethopyga siparaja	Crimson Sunbird
Rhipidura javanica	Pied Fantail	Arachnothera longirostra	Little Spiderhunter
Hypothymis azurea	Black-naped Monarch	Arachnothera crassirostri	Thick-billed Spiderhunter
Philentoma velatum	Maroon-breasted Flycatcher	Arachnothera flavigaster	Spectacled Spiderhunter
Philentoma pyrhopterum	Rufous-winged Flycatcher	Arachnothera chrysogenys	Yellow-eared Spiderhunter
Terpsiphone paradisi	Asian Paradise Flycatcher	Arachnothera affinis	Grey-breasted Spiderhunter
Motacilla cinerea	Grey Wagtail	Prionochilus maculatus	Yellow-breasted Flowerpecker
Motacilla flava	Yellow Wagtail	Prionochilus percussus	Crimson-breasted Flowerpecker
Dendronanthus indicus	Forest Wagtail	Dicaeum agile	Thick-billed Flowerpecker
Anthus hodgsoni	Olive-backed Pipit	Dicaeum chrysorrheum	Yellow-vented Flowerpecker
Anthus novaeseelandiae	Richard's Pipit	Dicaeum trigonostigma	Orange-bellied Flowerpecker
Anthus cervinus	Red-throated Pipit	Dicaeum cruentatum	Scarlet-backed Flowerpecker
Lanius cristatus	Brown Shrike	Zosterops palpebrosus	Oriental White -eye
Lanius tigrinus	Tiger Shrike	Zosterops everetti	Everett's White-eye
Aplonis panayensis	Philippine Glossy Starling	Paser montanus	Eurasian Tree sparrow
Sturnus sinensis	White-shouldered Starling	Passer flaveolus	Plain-backed Sparrow
Sturnus roseus	Rosy Starling	Ploceus philippinus	Baby Weaver
Sturnus contra	Pied Starling	Erythrura prasina	Pin-tailed Parrotfinch
Sturnus nigricollis	Black-collared Starling	Lonchura striata	White-rumped Munia
Sturnus burmannicus	Vinous-breasted Starling	Lonchura leucogastra	White-bellied Munia
Acridotheres tristis	Common Myna	Lonchura punctulata	Scaly-breasted Munia
Acridotheres javanicus	White-vented Myna	Lonchura maja	White-headed Munia
Ampeliceps coronatus	Golden-crested Myna		

B) MAMMAL SPECIES (EXPECTED / CONFIRMED) FROM KHAO SOK

Scientific Name	English Name	Scientific Name	English Name
Echinosorex gymnura	Moonrat	Taphozous melanopogon	Black-bearded Tomb Bat
Hylomys suillus	Pig-tailed Shrew	Nycteris tragata	Hollow-faced Bat
Suncus etruscus	Dwarf Shrew	Megaderma spasma	Lesser False Vampire Bat
Tupaia glis	Common Treeshrew	Rhinolophus malayanus	Malayan Horseshoe Bat
Tupaia minor	Lesser Treeshrew	Rhinolophus affinis	Intermediate Horseshoe Bat
Cynocephalus variegatus	Flying Lemur	Rhinolophus pusillus	Least Horseshoe Bat
Cynopterus brachyotis	Lesser Short-nosed Fruit Bat	Rhinolophus coelophyllus	Peters' Horseshoe Bat
Cynopterus sphinx	Great-short-nosed Fruit Bat	Rhinolophus trifoliatus	Treefoil Horseshoe Bat
Chironax melanocephalus	Black-capped Fruit Bat	Hipposideros bicolor	Bicolored Roundleaf Bat
Megaerops ecaudatus	Tailless Fruit Bat	Hipposideros cineraceus	Least Roundleaf Bat
Rousettus amplexicaudatus	Geoffroy's Rousette	Hipposideros lekaguli	Dr.Boonsong's Roundle Bat
Rousettus leschenaulti	Leschenault's Rousette	Hipposideros armiger	Great Roundleaf Bat
Pteropus vampyrus	Common Flying Fox	Hipposideros larvatus	Intermediate Roundle Bat
Macroglossus sobrinus	Great Long-tongued Flying Fox	Coelops frithi	E-A Tailless Roundle Bat
Eonycteris spelaea	Cave-dwelling Nectar-eating Bat	Myotis muricola	Whiskered Bat
Emballonura monticloa	Sheath-tailed Bat	Myotis hasseltii	Large-footed Bat
Taphozous longimanus	Long-winged Tomb bat	Pipistrellus javanicus	Javan Pipistrelle Bat

Scientific Name	English Name	Scientific Name	English Name
☐ Glischropus tylopus	Thick-thumbed Pipist Bat	☐ Tragulus napu	Greater Mouse Deer
☐ Tylonycteris pachypus	Lesser Club-footed Bat	☐ Tragulus javanicus	Lesser Mouse Deer
☐ Tylonycteris robustula	Greater Club-footed Bat	☐ Muntiacus muntjak	Barking Deer
☐ Hesperoptenus blanfordi	Blanford's Bat	☐ Muntiacus feae	Feae's Muntjak
☐ Scotophilus kuhlii	Lesser Yellow Bat	☐ Cervus unicolor	Sambar Deer
☐ Miniopterus schreibersi	Greater Bent-winged Bat	☐ Bos javanicus	Banteng
☐ Murina cyclotis	Tube-nosed Bat	☐ Bos gaurus	Gaur
☐ Kerivoula hardwickei	Hardwicke's Bat	☐ Capricornis sumatraensis	Serow
☐ Kerivoula picta	Painted Bat	☐ Manis javanica	Malay Pangolin
☐ Chaerephon plicata	Wrinkled-lipped Bat	☐ Ratufa bicolor	Black Giant Squirrel
☐ Nycticebus coucang	Slow Loris	☐ Ratufa affinis	Cream Giant Squirrel
☐ Macaca nemestrina	Pig-tail Macaque	☐ Callosciurus notatus	Plantain Squirrel
☐ Macaca arctoides	Stump-tailed Macaque	☐ Callosciurus flavimanus	Belly-banded Squirrel
☐ Macaca fascicularis	Long-tail Macaque	☐ Callosciurus caniceps	Grey-bellied Squirrel
☐ Presbytis melalophos	Banded Leaf-monkey	☐ Callosciurus prevosti	Prevost's Squirrel
☐ Presbytis obscura	Dusky Leaf-monkey	☐ Sundasciurus tenuis	Slender Squirrel
☐ Hylobates lar	Lar Gibbon	☐ Tamiops macclellandi	Burmese Striped Tree Squirrel
☐ Homo sapiens	Man	☐ Menetes berdmorei	Indochinese Ground Squirrel
☐ Cuon alpinus	Dhole/Wild Dog	☐ Rhinosciurus laticaudatus	Shrew-faced Ground Squirrel
☐ Ursus thibetanus	Asiatic Black Bear	☐ Petaurista elegans	Lesser Giant Flying Squirrel
☐ Helarctos malayanus	Malay Sunbear	☐ Petaurista petaurista	Red Giant Flying Squirrel
☐ Mustela nudipes	Malayan Weasel	☐ Aeromys tephromelas	Large Black Flying Squirrel
☐ Martes flavigula	Yellow-throated Marten	☐ Hylopetes lepidus	Red-cheeked Flying Squirrel
☐ Arctonyx collaris	Hog-Badger	☐ Petinomys setosus	White-bellied Flying Squirrel
☐ Melogale personata	Burmese Ferret-Badger	☐ Rhizomys sumatraensis	Large Bamboo Rat
☐ Lutra sumatrana	Hairy-nosed Otter	☐ Cannomys badius	Bay Bamboo Rat
☐ Aonyx cinerea	Small-clawed Otter	☐ Chiropodomys gliroides	Pencil-tail Tree Mouse
☐ Viverricula indica	Small Indian Civet	☐ Berylmys bowersi	Bowers' Rat
☐ Viverra zibetha	Large Indian Civet	☐ Maxomys whiteheadi	Whitehead's Rat
☐ Viverra megaspila	Large-spotted Civet	☐ Maxomys surifer	Yellow Rajah Rat
☐ Prionodon linsang	Banded Linsang	☐ Niviventer cremoriventer	Pencil-tailed Rat
☐ Arctogalidia trivirgata	Three striped Palm Civet	☐ Niviventer bukit	Chestnut Rat
☐ Paradoxurus hermaphroditu	Common Palm Civet	☐ Rattus argentiventer	Ricefield Rat
☐ Paguma larvata	Masked Palm Civet	☐ Rattus rattus	Roof Rat
☐ Arctictis binturong	Binturong	☐ Sundamys muelleri	Muller's Rat
☐ Hemigalus derbyanus	Banded Palm-civet	☐ Leopoldamys sabanus	Noisy Rat
☐ Cynogale bennetti	Other Civet	☐ Hystrix brachyuran	Malayan Porcupine
☐ Herpestes javanicus	Javan Mongoose	☐ Atherurus macrourus	Brush-tail Porcupine
☐ Herpestes urva	Crabeating Mongoose		
☐ Pardofelis marmorata	Marbled Cat		
☐ Prionailurus viverrina	Fishing Cat		
☐ Prionailurus bengalensis	Leopard Cat		
☐ Catopuma temmincki	Golden Cat		
☐ Neofelis nebulosa	Clouded Leopard		
☐ Panthera pardus	Leopard		
☐ Panthera tigris	Tiger		
☐ Elephas maximus	Elephant		
☐ Tapirus indicus	Malay Tapir		
☐ Dicerorhinus sumatrensis	Sumatran Rhinceros		
☐ Sus scrofa	Common Wild Pig		

C) REPTILE SPECIES (EXPECTED/CONFIRMED) FROM KHAO SOK

Scientific Name	English Name	Scientific Name	English Name
Heosemys grandis	Giant Asian Pond Turtle	Naja naja	Asiatic Spitting Cobra
Cyclemys dentatea	Asian Leaf Turtle	Naja kaouthia	Monocellate Cobra
Manouria emys	Asian Brown Tortoise	Ophiophagus hannah	King Cobra
Indotestudo elongata	Elongated Tortoise	Aplopeltura boa	Blunt-headed Slug Snake
Trionyx subplanus	Malayan Softshell Turtle	Homalopsis buccata	Puff-faced Water Snake
Trionyx formosus	Burmese Paecock Softshell Turtle	Amphiesma groundwateri	Groundwater's Keelback
Trionyx cartilagineus	Asiatic Softshell Turtle	Xenochrophis piscator	Checkered Keelback
Cyrtodactylus brevipalmat	Webbed-toed Forest Gecko	Xenochrophis flavipunctat	Common Keelback
Cyrtodactylus pulchellus	Malayan Banded Gecko	Rhabdophis subminiatus	Red-necked Keelback
Cyrtodactylus oldhami	Oldham's Forest Gecko	Rhabdophis nigrocinctus	Green Keelback
Cyrtodactylus peguensis	Pegu Forest Gecko	Gonyosoma oxycephalum	Red-tailed Racer
Cnemaspis siamensis	Siamese Dwarf Gecko	Elaphe taeniura	Stripe-tailed Racer
Hemidactylus frenatus	Common House Gecko	Elaphe radiata	Copperhead Racer
Hemidactylus garnotii	Pale House Gecko	Ptyas korros	Indochinese Rat Snake
Cosymbotus platyurus	Common Flat-tailed Gecko	Zaocys carinatus	Keeled Rat Snake
Gekko gecko	Tokay Gecko	Dendrelaphis pictus	Painted Bronzeback
Ptychozoon lionatum	Common Flying Gecko	Boiga cyanea	Green Cat Snake
Draco maculatus	Orange-winged Flying Lizard	Boiga dendrophila	Mangrove Snake
Draco valans	Common Flying Lizard	Boiga cynodon	Dog-toothed Cat Snake
Draco taeniopterrus	Banded-winged Flying Lizard	Ahaetulla prasina	Oriental Whip Snake
Acanthosaura armata	Greater Spiny Lizard	Ahaetulla mycterizans	Malayan Green Whip Snake
Acanthosaura crucigera	Lesser Spiny Lizard	Dryophiops rubescens	Red Whip Snake
Calotes cristatellus	Green Lizard	Psammodynastes pulverulen	Common Mock Viper
Calotes versicolor	Red-headed Lizard	Chrysopelea paradisi	Paradise Tree Snake
Calotes mystaceus	Garden Blue Lizard	Chrysopelea ornata	Common Tree Snake
Calotes emma	Forest Lizard	Lycodon laoensis	Indochinese Wolf Snake
Leiolepis belliana	Granular-scaled Lizard	Lycodon capucinus	Common Wolf Snake
Varanus rudicollis	Black Jungle Monitor	Oligodon cyclurus	Common Kukri Snake
Varanus dumerilii	Red-headed Monitor	Liopeltis scriptus	Common Ringneck Snake
Varanus salvator	Common Water Monitor	Dryocalamus davisonii	Common Bridle Snake
Varanus bengalwnsis	Bengal Monitor	Calloselasma rhodostoma	Malayan Pit Viper
Takydromus sexlineatus	Six-lined Grass Lizard	Trimeresurus purpureomacu	Shore Pit Viper
Dasia loivacea	Olivaceous Tree Skink	Trimeresurus kanburiensis	Kanburi Pit Viper
Mabuya macularia	Variable Skink	Trimeresurus popeorum	Pope's Pit Viper
Mabuya multifasciata	Common Asiatic Skink	Trimeresurus sumatranus	Sumatran Pit Viper
Mabuya longicaudata	Long-tailed Skink	Trimeresurus hageni	Hagen's Pit Viper
Lygosoma boweingi	Common Supple Skink	Trimeresurus wagleri	Wagler's Pit Viper
Sphenomorphus maculatus	Common Hill Skink		
Sphenomorphus tersus	Pale Hill Skink		
Lipinia vittigera	Common Striped Skink		
Tropidophorus robinsoni	Robinson's Stream Skink		
Typhlops diardi	Indochinese Blind Snake		
Acrochordus javanicus	Javan Wart Snake		
Acrochordus grandulatus	Asiatic File Snake		
Python reticulatus	Reticulated Python		
Python curtus	Blood Python		
Maticora bivirgata	Blue Malaysian C. Snake		
Bungarus flaviceps	Red-headed Krait		
Bungarus candidus	Malayan Krait		
Bungarus fasciatus	Banded Krait		

D) AMPHIBIA SPECIES (EXPECTED/CONFIRMED) FROM KHAO SOK

Scientific Name	English Name
☐ Megophrys aceras	Lesser Horned Toad
☐ Bufo asper	Malayan Giant Toad
☐ Bufo melanostictus	Common Asiatic Toad
☐ Bufo Parvus	Straight-ridged Toad
☐ Phrynoglossus laevis	Common Puddle Frog
☐ Phrynoglossus martensi	Paddyfield Puddle Frog
☐ Amolops larutensis	Malayan Torren Frog
☐ Rana erythraea	Paddyfield Green Frog
☐ Rana alticola	Brown Hill Frog
☐ Rana miopus	Oblique-striped Frog
☐ Rana nigrovittata	Common Brown Frog
☐ Rana chalconota	Copper-cheeked Frog
☐ Rana hosii	Malayan Cascade Frog
☐ Rana glandulosa	Glandular Frog
☐ Rana signata	Yellow-spotted Frog

Scientific Name	English Name
☐ Rana rugulosa	Common Lowland Frog
☐ Rana limocharis	Marsh Frog
☐ Rana blythii	Malayan Giant Frog
☐ Ingerana tasanae	Smith's Wrinkled Frog
☐ Rhacophorus bimaculatus	Blue-legged Flying Frog
☐ Rhacophorus nigropalmatus	Wallace's Flying Frog
☐ Rhacophorus leucomystax	Common Bush Frog
☐ Kaloula baleata	Malaysian Burrowing Frog
☐ Microhyla berdmorei	Hour-glass Froglet
☐ Microhyla borneensis	Bornean Froglet
☐ Microhyla butleri	Noisy Froglet
☐ Microhyla heymonsi	Dark-sided Froglet
☐ Microhyla ornata	Ornata Froglet
☐ Micryletta inornata	Inornate Froglet

COMMON WILDLIFE TRACKS AT KHAO SOK

Jungle fowl

Long-tailed macaque

Monitor Lizard

Otter

Malay sun bear

Leopard

(NOTE: Animals not drawn to scale)

COMMON WILDLIFE TRACKS AT KHAO SOK

Porcupine

Civet

Mouse deer

F H

Tiger

Wild pig

Pig-tail macaque

Elephant

Tapir

(NOTE: Animals not drawn to scale)

BIBLIOGRAPHY

Bernard, Hans-Ulrich "Insight Guides Southeast Asia Wildlife".
APA Publications (HK) Ltd., Singapore, 1991

Boonsong Lekagul : Mc Neely, Jeffrey a, "Mammals of Thailand".
Darnsutha Press, Bangkok, 1988

Cubitt Gerald, Stewart-Cox Belinda "Wild Thailand". Asia Books,
Bangkok; 1995

Davison, Geoffrey W.H. "Endau Rompin-A Malaysian Heritage".
Malayan Nature Society, Kuala Lumpur ; 1988

Dickinson, Edward C. & King, Ben F. "A Field Guide to the Birds of South -
East Asia". Collins, London ; 1975

Eve Roland, Guigue Anne-Marie "Birds of Thailand", Times Editions Pte Ltd.
Singapore; 1996

Fres Paul, Smart "The Illustrated Encyclopedia of the Butterfly World in Color".
Hamlyn Publishing Group Ltd., London; 1976

Graham, Mark, Gray, Denis & Piprell, Collins "National Parks of Thailand."
Communication Resources (Thailand) Ltd., Bangkok ; 1991

Graham Mark, Round Phillip "Thailand's Vanishing Flora and Fauna"
Finance One Public Co., Ltd., Bangkok; 1994

Lees Paul "The Dive Sites of Thailand". Asia Books, Bangkok; 1995

Mitchell, Andrew W. "The Emerald Canopy - Secrets From the Rainforest Roof".
Fontana/Collins, Great Britain ; 1986

Piancharoen Charoen "Geologic Resources of Thailand : Potential for Future Development",
Department of Mineral Resources, Bangkok; 1992

Rubeli, Ken "Tropical Rainforest of South - East Asia - A pictorial Journey".
Tropical Press SDN.BHD, Kuala Lumpur ; 1986

Tem Smitinand. "Wild Flowers of Thailand". Self published, Bangkok ; 1975

Van Beek, Steve. "Thailands Natural Heritage". Thai Air International,
Hongkong ; 1992

Van Strien Nico "A Guide to the Tracks of the Mammals of Western Indonesia".
School of Environmental Conservation Management,
Bogor, Indonesia; 1983

ACKNOWLEDGEMENTS

There are a number of people to whom I am deeply indebted for sharing with me over the past decade their extensive knowledge of the Southeast Asian rainforest. My heartfelt thanks to: Dawat Lupung and Mutang Tuo, Penan friends from Sarawak, Borneo, and to Bokolo, Mikoll, Aleko, Aman Ubet Keri, Mati Keri, Gejeng and Sarul, my dear Mentawai friends on the island of Siberut, Indonesia for many years of entrusting me with the secrets of their forests and their tribal ways.

I wish to thank the late Bruno Manser for his many insights, Anisak Chanyoo (Nit), and Khun Choy, Khao Sok master guides and rainforest professors who know more about this forest than any academic on Earth.

I want to acknowledge the authors of the books listed in the bibliography for their comprehensive and authoritative information. I am especially grateful to Jo Hardman, a young scientist from Liverpool, England, for her invaluable work compiling and translating information on Khao Sok, and to Dr. Tony Lynman from the University of California for sharing with me his research findings based on five years at Khao Sok. I am indebted to both Jo and Tony and to Dr. Bristol Foster for reviewing and critiquing this manuscript.

Finally, I want to express profound appreciation for the Thai Kingdom's foresight in protecting a national and global treasure as priceless as Khao Sok.